Developing Individualized Family Support Plans

A TRAINING MANUAL

By Tess Bennett, Barbara V. Lingerfelt and Donna E. Nelson

BROOKLINE

Library of Congress Cataloging-in-Publication Data

Bennett, Tess
      Developing individualized family support plans / Tess Bennett,
Barbara Lingerfelt, and Donna Nelson.
     p.   cm.
     Includes bibliographical references.
     ISBN 0-914797-69-7
     1. Social work with handicapped children--Study and teaching-
-United States. 2. Family social work--Study and teaching--United
States. 3. Social workers--In-service training--United States.
I. Lingerfelt, Barbara. II. Nelson, Donna. III. Title.
     [DNLM: 1. Child, Preschool--education--United States.
2. Education, Special--United States. 3. Family. 4. Handicapped.
5. Social Work--United States. HV 3001 B472w]
HV888.5.B46 1990
362.4'043'083--dc20
DNLM/DLC
for Library of Congress   90-1378
                                   CIP

Published by

Brookline Books

P.O. Box 1046, Cambridge, MA 02238-1046

*"You can't help men permanently by doing for them
what they could and should do for themselves."*

--Abraham Lincoln

Acknowledgments

We would like to thank our colleagues and friends who contributed greatly to the development of this training manual. First, we would like to recognize the work of our colleagues, Carl Dunst, Carol Trivette, and Angela Deal, at the Family, Infant and Preschool Program. Their contributions to the field over the years have been extremely important. Their book, *Enabling and Empowering Families,* provided the basis for much of this training manual.

We would like to acknowledge case coordinators, Family Place Staff, Family Enablement Staff, and the staff of other FIPP projects for their invaluable contributions.

We would like to thank Steffi Adams, Lynda Pletcher, and Alma Davis for their help.

We would like to thank Maye Hardin and Beth Woods, instructional design consultants, who contributed greatly to the construction of this training manual.

We would like to thank trainees in the Family Specialist Training Program who participated in all phases of the training and provided valuable feedback on training content and methods.

The Family Specialist Training Program, which carried out training seminars, application and follow-up visits was supported by a grant from the U.S. Department of Education, Office of Special Education Programs (G008730267).

Preface

It is no accident that training about the Individualized Family Support Plan (IFSP) was developed at the Family, Infant and Preschool Program (FIPP) in Morganton, North Carolina. FIPP began in 1972 and has been involved with over 1400 families with young handicapped children, providing family support through home-based and center-based programs. All activities at FIPP, including the research and training, are guided by the following mission, which was articulated by a group of parents and professionals involved in the program.

"To support and strengthen families in ways that enhance their growth and well-being. Growth and well-being are enhanced by creating opportunities that promote the competence of the family and individual family members to meet their needs and achieve their goals. Competency-building is accomplished through partnerships between parents and professionals based upon respect, trust, and compassion. The commitment to supporting and strengthening family functioning guides all activities of the Family, Infantand Preschool Program, including direct service, model-demonstration, training and technical assistance, and research and evaluation."

(Mission Statement, Family, Infant and Preschool Program, 1989)

In carrying out this mission, FIPP staff have been developing the equivalent of IFSP's for several years.

The staff of the Family Specialist Training Program (FSTP), located at FIPP, developed this manual. FSTP is a Handicapped Children's Early Education Program (HCEEP) Inservice Training Project for professionals working with infants. The project was funded to deliver on-site training and develop high-quality training materials for national dissemination. This training project was consistent with FIPP philosophy in all aspects of training and product development. The training methods described in the manual have been field-tested over a period of two years. Enhanced training effects are possible by utilizing the materials and methods discussed in the manual. The project is in the third year of funding at the time of this printing and beginning a very thorough project evaluation. Results of the evaluation can be obtained by writing the authors. It is the hope of the authors that this training manual will be a useful guide to trainers, administrators, help-giving professionals, and supervisors who are involved in family-centered intervention for families with handicapped infants and toddlers.

Table of Contents

The Effective Help-Giver

Writing Family Support Plans

Case Studies

Appendices

References

Introduction

Since the passage of P.L. 99-457, the field of early childhood special education has entered a new era. One element of this new era is the recognized role of the family in the care and education of the handicapped infant or toddler. P.L. 99-457 is one of the first pieces of national legislation in recent history to articulate strong support of families. The most salient feature of the law, which demonstrates this support, is the Individualized Family Support Plan (IFSP). The IFSP includes information about family needs, strengths and resources. These components of the IFSP attest to the positive framework which P.L. 99-457 provides to families and professionals. The IFSP is designed to be developed in partnership with the family. The family's role is very active in carrying out mutually developed goals.

This focus on partnerships with family members brings attention to the need for well-trained professionals who have the ability to form partnerships in working with families with handicapped infants and toddlers, particularly in developing the IFSP. There is a great need for information and high-quality competency-based training which is founded on sound adult-learning principles for professionals who are asked to perform new roles in their daily work.

Who is the training manual for?

This training manual is for anyone responsible for training, e.g., inservice training coordinators, agency administrators, supervisors and university personnel. The manual can be used either for group training or for self-study. This manual is designed to be used with the text *Enabling and Empowering Families: Principles and Guidelines for Practice* by Dunst, Trivette, and Deal. It is available form Brookline Books, P. O. Box 1046, Cambridge, MA, 02238-1046.

How is this material different from other material?

Using P.L. 99-457 as a guideline, the staff of the Family, Infant and Preschool Program have designed a functional and useful approach to developing IFSP's. The IFSP is viewed from a specific philosophical framework which encompasses both the requirements of legislation and FIPP's commitment to helping families learn to help themselves. The material presented on IFSP's in this manual is substantive, yet easy to understand and practical to use.

What is included in the manual?

Everything the trainer needs is included; notes on preparing for the training, content for the seminar, a thorough list of competencies (Appendix A), a training checklist (Appendix B), portfolio activities (Appendix C), a blank set of assessment and IFSP forms (Appendix D), overhead masters (Appendix E), and a glossary of terms (Appendix F). A list of references for additional study is also included.

The IFSP content is broken down into eight sequential sections so the material can be assimilated easily and trainers can build a sound, logical knowledge base. The culminating activity is an exercise in constructing a case study and writing a practice IFSP. The IFSP format presented in the manual represents the efforts of many FIPP staff members to simplify and streamline paperwork. All of the activities have been field-tested and reworked to ensure usability and maximize the potential for experiential change through training.

How is this manual organized?

The rationale for IFSP is provided in the first section of the manual. The next sections include: Working with Families, Needs and Aspirations, Strengths and Capabilities, Support and Resources, The Effective Help-Giver, and Writing Family Support Plans. The last section of the manual contains case studies which provide simple, concrete examples of families with young handicapped children and an activity which asks the trainee to write a short case study and IFSP on a familiar family. Each section is organized internally in the following consistent fashion:

- "Trainer's Notes" -- lists necessary equipment, discussion questions and tips for leading discussions, as well as gives time estimates and instructions for activities; can be located by the black tab in the upper right hand corner of the page.

- "Points to Look For" -- previews important points, lists discussion questions and provides space for notes.

- Text -- contains subject matter content and seminar activities (entitled "Stop and Practice Your Skills").

- "Tips from the Text" and "Section Checklists" -- review the major points just presented.

Where should I begin?

Trainers should begin by reading the General Trainer's Notes (following this introduction), then proceed through the manual in sequence. Special attention should be given to the section-specific Trainer's Notes at the beginning of each section.

Participants in the training should read the content sections of the manual in the sequence they are presented. The readings should be completed prior to the training session in order to make the most efficient use of group discussion time.

General Trainer's Notes

Trainer's Notes

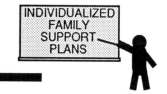

How is adult learning different from children's learning?

Research on adult learning provides a theoretical basis for the use of adult learning strategies (Knowles, 1979, 1978), since adults learn differently from children. There are four crucial assumptions that differentiate adults from children as learners:

- The adult's self-concept moves from dependency to self-direction.

- The adult accumulates a growing reservoir of experience that becomes an increasing resource for learning.

- The adult's readiness to learn becomes oriented increasingly to the developmental tasks of his or her social roles.

- The adult's time perspective changes from one of postponed application of knowledge to immediacy of application. Accordingly, his or her orientation toward learning shifts from subject centeredness to problem centeredness (Sakata, 1984).

What training strategies work well with adult learners?

- Use concrete study materials. The case study approach, utilizing both written and visual materials is very useful. The immediate application of material helps promote meaningfulness and recall.

- Independent readings are useful only if there is time for reflective discussion. Readings need to be adapted to the level of the trainee.

- Group experiences provide opportunities for information exchange and facilitate learning. Most adult learners find this helpful.

- Self-growth is of great interest to the adult learner. Learning experiences which contribute to overall growth help the adult assimilate knowledge.

- Learning style is an important factor in training adults. Ward (1983) identified four learning styles: idealistic, pragmatic, realistic, and existentialistic. Adults do not usually fall into only one category, but may have strong characteristics of one or more styles. Teachers of adult learners need to note that these individual learning styles will affect how adults assimilate material.

- Internal motivation is present in many adult learners because they are self-directed. Adults like to make their own decisions and be autonomous in the learning process.

- The use of a variety of instructional methods is important if training is to be effective. It is suggested that at least three different techniques be used within a given training session for optimal learning to occur. An example of this would be the use of discussion, demonstration and small group activities.

What is the ideal schedule for training?

For the most effective training, we suggest a format similar to the two illustrated below. Option A is the basic outline, while Option B includes an additional follow-up session. This comprehensive training design, based on much experience in training professionals, enables trainees to gain knowledge, build skills on that knowledge and demonstrate new skills and behaviors. Opportunities for individual and group interaction are optimal for learning and consistent with adult learning theory.

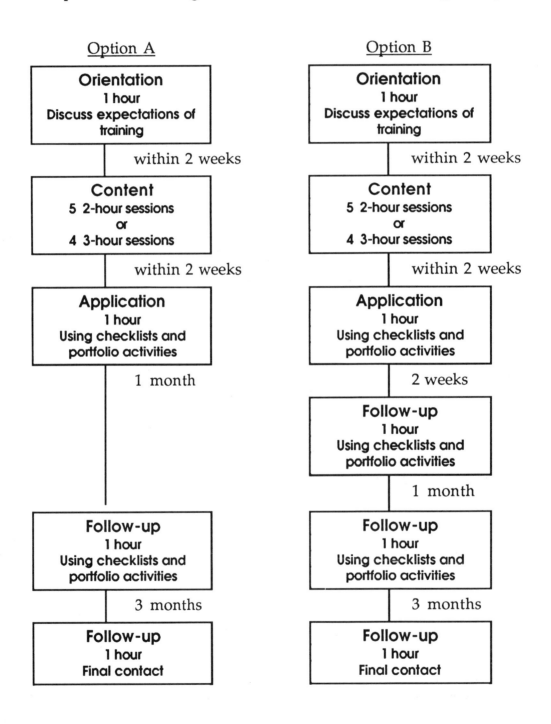

The material in the content sessions of the training manual takes a total of about 10-12 hours to present if the trainees have access to the training manual and read the manual ahead of time. The training manual is also suitable for a standard ten-hour workshop for one continuing education credit. Content may be covered in four three-hour sessions (as illustrated below) or five two-hour sessions. The final case study assignment might be done as homework. If the trainer chooses to maximize the training experience, the authors suggest using the checklists and portfolio activities. Even though this will add approximately 3 hours of training time, skill acquisition will improve with this addition.

If the trainer is not available to make site visits to trainees or if there are time restrictions for the trainer, trainees can be paired in teams. These teams of peers may play the role of mentor or coach for one another. They can support each other, discuss checklists and carry out portfolio activities together. This is a cost-effective way to build in follow-up.

If content sessions are each 3 hours, here is an example of the way topics could be presented per session:

Session 1
    Introduction/Law/Rationale
    Working with Families
    Needs and Aspirations

Session 2
    Strengths and Capabilities

Session 3
    Support and Resources

Session 4
    The Effective Help-Giver
    Writing IFSP's
    Case Studies (may be done as homework)

Seminar discussion, checklist training, mentoring/coaching, opportunities for immediate feedback, use of concrete examples and the use of the case study approach are consistent with adult learning theory and help adults assimilate content. If possible, it is optimal to meet prior to the seminar to discuss needs and expectations of trainees in regard to the training. The content seminar should not be a lecture, but a true discussion time. Example discussion questions are provided in the Trainer's Notes. Within 2 weeks, one-on-one application visits with trainer or mentor and several follow-up visits, at the trainee's program, spaced about a month apart are suggested.

The competency listing (Appendix A) provides the knowledge-based and performance-based framework for the material in the training manual. The authors suggest trainers begin by reviewing the list with trainees as an advance organizer. A competency-based approach includes using the checklist (Appendix B) during the application and follow-up visits. The next section of this introduction discusses two techniques which can be used during visits to the trainee's site to extend skill levels. These two techniques are checklist training and completion of portfolio activities.

Checklist Training

The checklist in Appendix B may be used during the one-on-one application and during follow-up visits to assess and maintain performance. A checklist is a very efficient and cost-effective training method. The process of using a checklist is as follows. The trainer first shares the checklist with the trainee and discusses it. Next, the trainer may model the behavior for the trainee. The trainer then observes the trainee carrying out the activity, or reviews the activity, gives feedback, and makes suggestions for future success. The observation and feedback steps are repeated until the desired level of performance is achieved. These steps may be repeated over time to maintain performance. A rule of thumb the authors used was to bring all trainees to 90% criterion on checklists to attain competence.

One potential problem with using checklists is that if they are presented as tests, they may result in negative feedback. At best, checklist training promotes communication and positive feedback. It is an effective training method that requires little time and is widely used to train professionals.

Giving feedback when using a checklist is important. Feedback refers to the systematic process of communicating with a person about his/her actions or performance. Feedback is an essential part of most learning strategies, e.g., simulation, coaching, mentoring, modeling, and demonstration. Feedback is much more effective when used consistently with another training strategy such as a checklist. It is important to ask the person before receiving feedback how he/she feels about his/her performance. Also, it is helpful to give positive feedback first and then give negative feedback after the positive comments.

Portfolio Activities

Portfolio activities are practical exercises which enable trainees to practice a skill learned in class. Portfolio activities are designed to be carried out in an on-the-job fashion. Feedback is also an important element of portfolio activities. These activities can be assigned before application and then discussed at follow-up visits. It is beneficial for trainers to spend time one-on-one with trainees to review and give practical feedback on portfolio activities.

The authors suggest trainers incorporate all activities provided in the text, review the competency listing in Appendix A, use the checklist in Appendix B and portfolio activities in Appendix C. A blank set of assessment and IFSP forms are provided in Appendix D. These can be used for further practice activities and case studies. Overhead transparencies masters for seminar are provided in Appendix E.

The use of all of these training materials in the sequence suggested earlier will ensure a comprehensive training plan which will provide optimal conditions for learning the process of developing IFSP's.

Preparing for the Seminar Session

- Use overhead transparency masters in Appendix E to create transparencies, if you plan to use them in seminar.

- Read the entire section of the manual before beginning seminar.

- Familiarize yourself with the discussion questions.

- If possible, review other materials referred to in the manual.

- Practice completing activities.

- Be sure that the overhead projector, if you plan to use it, is working properly, has a good light bulb (a spare bulb is a good idea, too!), and is placed so that projections are not blocked.

- Arrange seating so that all trainees can see the screen while still being grouped to facilitate discussion.

P.L. 99-457

PUBLIC LAW 99-457: A RATIONALE FOR THE IFSP

This training manual examines the basis of the Individualized Family Service Plan, as well as factors to consider and methods to employ when putting this plan into action. It is helpful at this point, however, to briefly look at the law which initiated the development of the IFSP.

Public Law 99-457, Part H

Education of the Handicapped Amendments of 1986 (Public Law 99-457) provides new incentives for the development of services to young handicapped children and their families.

Part H of the statute establishes support and guidance to early intervention programs designed to meet the special needs of handicapped infants and toddlers and their families. Development of an Individualized Family Service Plan (IFSP) has provided a means for guiding resource mobilization to meet child and family needs.

The framers of the legislation intended that families themselves become key participants in the development of IFSP's. The partnership between parents and professionals helps parents gain the knowledge and skills necessary to utilize support systems to strengthen family functioning.

Major New Initiatives

Below is a brief summary of the major new initiatives of P.L. 99-457, including (in italics) the initiative upon which early intervention programs for handicapped infants and toddlers and their families is based.

- Extends P.L. 94-142 to age three by school year 1990-91.
- *Creates new state grant program for handicapped infants and toddlers (birth through age two -- full services in four years.)*
- Strengthens P.L. 94-142 interagency provisions.
- Establishes expanded authority on technology, media, and materials for the handicapped.
- Creates a National Center on Recruitment and Employment in Special Education.

Individualized Family Service Plan

One of the requirements of the Early Intervention Program initiative of the recently enacted P.L. 99-457 (Part H) is the Individualized Family Service Plan (IFSP). According to the *Congressional Record* (1986, p.H7895), the IFSP must contain:

1. a statement of the child's present levels of development (cognitive, speech/language, psychosocial, motor, and self-help)
2. a statement of the family's strengths and needs relating to enhancing the child's development
3. a statement of major outcomes expected to be achieved for the child and family and the criteria, procedures, and timelines for determining progress
4. the specific early intervention services necessary to meet the unique needs of the child and family
5. projected dates for initiation of services and expected duration
6. the name of the case manager who will be responsible for the implementation of the plan
7. procedures for transition from early intervention into a pre-school program

The IFSP must be developed from child and family assessments conducted by a multidisciplinary team. The team needs to include at least one of the child's parents or the child's guardian. The IFSP needs to be reviewed at least once a year and parents are to receive a progress report on the IFSP every six months.

It is not important for you to learn these seven components of the IFSP at this point in this workshop, since these components will be examined in more detail later.

Family Service Plans vs. Family Support Plans

The following sections of this manual will examine the Individualized Family Service Plan, and look at the family-centered approach developed by the staff of the Family, Infant and Preschool Program at the Western Carolina Center in Morganton, North Carolina.

To distinguish between these two versions of the IFSP, we will use the term "Individualized Family <u>Service</u> Plan" to refer to the version described in PL 99-457 and "Individualized Family <u>Support</u> Plan" to refer to the version developed by the FIPP staff. The use of the word support instead of services denotes an emphasis on enabling the family through encouragement and support, rather than an emphasis on the "service" of solving the family's problems.

Working With Families

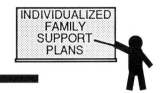

Trainer's Notes

Working with families is a complex, challenging, and rewarding task. No two families are alike, nor are their needs or the personal resources they bring to daily living. Yet with all this diversity, there are some basic principles upon which effective work with families can be based.

Working with Families provides the theoretical bases upon which this training is founded. This section also contains statements which will preview the content of the following sections.

At the end of this section are four goals for conducting family-level assessments and interventions. Achievement of these goals will be demonstrated by the successful completion of the Individualized Family Support Plan at the end of the manual.

Time

For a training group of 10 people, allow 1 hour to discuss this section, answer questions, and complete any exercises or activities.

Materials

For this session you will need to have:
- training manual for *Developing Individualized Family Support Plans*
- *Enabling and Empowering Families* (Dunst, Trivette & Deal, 1988)
- chalkboard and chalk or newsprint and markers, along with masking tape to attach pieces of newsprint to the wall
- optional: overhead transparencies
- optional: overhead projector and screen or light-colored wall

Before You Begin

- Be sure all equipment is set up properly.
- Read the material in the manual on **Working with Families**.
- Be prepared to discuss the questions on the next page.

Discussion Questions

❑ Viewing a family from a social systems perspective involves consideration of the formal and informal social units who influence and are influenced by the family. *Why is this a more realistic approach to take when working with families in need than to focus solely on the family?*

❑ The roles of the help-seekers (family) and the help-giver are interdependent in the model presented here. *How do these roles differ from the ones you are most familiar with?*

❑ Five key principles upon which this family-based model depends are presented from the viewpoint of the help-giver. *How will you have to adapt your methods for working with families in order to use and build upon these principles?*

❑ In this section we present a set of guidelines for conducting a successful assessment interview with a family. *What methods can you use to incorporate these guidelines into your present way of working with families so they become familiar and easy to use?*

Tips for Leading Discussion

• Ask for specific questions from the reading and try to involve other group members in suggesting answers.

• Encourage discussion by asking, "How would you explain the theories stated here to someone from your office/agency who could not attend the training?"

• Ask trainees if they believe this approach to working with families will make more work for them because they will relinquish the authority to set and limit the agenda? Encourage them to talk about their concerns. Reinforce the goal of helping families become ultimately self-sustaining as a way not only to strengthen the families but also to limit the direct services the help giver must provide.

• Emphasize the concepts of <u>empowering,</u> <u>enabling,</u> <u>strengthening,</u> and <u>enhancing</u> the acquisition of skills during discussion. Reassure trainees that the "How To" part of developing these concepts will be thoroughly addressed in the upcoming sections of this module.

• Encourage trainees to discuss the differences between the ways they now interact with families and the ways suggested in this reading. <u>Support</u> anyone willing to share personal experiences that emphasize these differences.

• If trainees are reluctant to talk about themselves, be prepared to share an experience of your own to illustrate your change in approach to working with families since this training.

Points to Look For

Working with families is a complex, challenging, and rewarding task. No two families are alike, nor are their needs or the personal resources they bring to daily living. Yet with all this diversity, there are some basic principles upon which effective work with families can be based.

This section of the training manual, entitled **Working with Families**, will provide you with the theoretical bases upon which this training is founded. At the end of this section you will be presented with four goals for conducting family-level assessments and interventions. Achievement of these goals will be demonstrated by the successful completion of the Individualized Family Support Plan.

Listed below are some important points to look for and remember as you read. You can use the back of this page to make your own notes or responses to the items below.

Discussion Questions

❑ Viewing a family from a social systems perspective involves consideration of the formal and informal social units who influence and are influenced by the family. *Why is this a more realistic approach to take when working with families in need than to focus solely on the family?*

❑ The roles of the help-seekers (family) and the help-giver are interdependent in the model presented here. *How do these roles differ from the ones you are most familiar with?*

❑ Five key principles upon which this family-based model depends are presented from the viewpoint of the help-giver. *How will you adapt your methods for working with families in order to use and build upon these principles?*

❑ This section presents a set of guidelines for conducting a successful assessment interview with a family. *What methods can you use to incorporate these guidelines into your present way of working with families so they become familiar and easy to use?*

Notes

WORKING WITH FAMILIES

Meeting the goal of this training -- successfully writing and implementing Individualized Family Support Plans -- requires specific efforts on the part of both the help-seeker and the help-giver. Determination of these efforts has occurred over time, after considerable research and experimentation. A proposed helping model, derived from the results of this theoretical and empirical evidence, is presented and summarized in *Enabling and Empowering Families* (Dunst, Trivette, & Deal, 1988), the text which accompanies this training manual.

An Enabling Model of Helping

This model of helping is referred to as an "enabling" model because the major role of the help-giver is to enable the development of skills and competencies leading to self-reliance and self-fulfillment on the part of the help-seeker. Under this model, help-seekers are assumed to possess, or to be capable of acquiring, the skills and competencies necessary to respond to life's challenges and demands when given the encouragement and the opportunities to do so.

Expectations of the Help-Seeker

This model of helping does not focus on the past or place emphasis on the help-seeker's responsibility for causing problems. It does, however, highly emphasize the help-seeker's responsibility for acquiring and using the skills and information necessary to meet present and future needs and goals. Help-seekers are expected to play a major role in supporting family projects, considering how they can go about meeting their needs, and determining what course of action will be taken to that end. **In other words, the help-seeker is the essential agent of change; the help-giver supports, encourages, and helps create opportunities for the help-seeker to achieve success.**

Expectations of the Help-Giver

As mentioned above, the help-giver assists the family (help-seekers) in determining their own agenda of needs and goals. The help-seeker also encourages and supports efforts on the family's part to meet their own needs and goals, while serving as a valuable resource for the family as they develop their own abilities. The help-giver's role is a positive one of helping the family as they identify their own strengths, develop their strengths more fully, and use their strengths effectively in their day-to-day lives.

This effort between help-seeker and help-giver is a partnership which emphasizes joint responsibility for developing the family's abilities to meet their own needs and achieve their own goals, not just now but also into the future.

Focus on the Family

Another hallmark of the model we present here is a focus on the entire family rather than just on the child whose condition or treatment has introduced the family to the help-giver. This approach is based on family systems theory -- a philosophy that focuses on interactions among family members rather individuals within a family.

The family systems approach believes the disabled child will be best served by focusing on the family and that help-givers have a responsibility to address the needs of all individuals in the family. Considering the family as the unit for intervention increases the likelihood that any changes made (e.g., needs met or goals achieved) will have a positive outcome for all family members.

Focusing on the family and enabling parents in their efforts to meet the needs of all family members (including themselves) is the most efficient way of developing parental skills which can enhance the well-being and development of all family members. Immediate and urgent needs will necessarily have priority. For example, if a family has no heat in the winter, the need for warmth must be met before attention can be turned to other child and family needs.

Because family systems theory is so important to the approach presented in this training, it is worthwhile to take a few minutes to be sure the basics of this philosophy are well understood.

Family Systems Theory

As was mentioned above, family systems theory is a philosophy that searches for the causes of behavior, not in the individual alone, but in the interactions among family members. This family systems approach is based on a model with four main components:

1. **Family Structure**: descriptive characteristics of the family, its membership and organization
2. **Family Interaction**: the way the family system interacts to meet individual member and collective family needs

3. **Family Functions**: activities the family engages in to meet its own needs (economic, affection, etc.)

4. **Family Life Cycle**: developmental and non-developmental changes that families pass through which alter family structure and family needs (Turnbull, Summers, & Brotherson, 1984)

Family interaction, which describes the way family members or sub-groups within the family interact with one another on a day-to-day basis, is the essential focus of the system. In order to understand family interaction it is necessary to understand that families consist of definable subsystems and that the rules of interaction among these subsystems are governed by the family's level of cohesion, its adaptability, and its communication style.

Family Subsystems

Four major subsystems are recognized by most family theorists as generally defining interactions within the nuclear family, although all subsystems are not present in all families. These subsystems include:

- marital -- husband/wife interactions
- parental -- child/parent interactions
- sibling -- child/child interactions; may be further subdivided in families with many children
- extrafamilial -- family or individual interactions with extended family, friends, community, etc.

Individual family members play different roles in different subsystems. Subsystem boundaries are defined by the unspoken rules that let family members know how to behave within a given subsystem. Clearly defined boundaries that still permit flexibility are standard in balanced families.

It is important to remember, though, that even in families where the boundaries are extremely rigid, anything that happens in one subsystem affects the other subsystems and individuals.

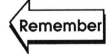

Cohesion

Cohesion is the degree of closeness (or distance) among family members, the emotional bonding they have for one another. Personal independence, or individual autonomy within the family system, provides a balance for family cohesion.

In a positive sense, cohesion can be thought of as the family's ability to maintain unity and simultaneously allow for individuation. Families lacking unity are termed disengaged while families whose members lack individual autonomy are described as enmeshed. Measurable indicators of cohesion are (Turnbull, Summers, & Brotherson, 1984):

- closeness -- the feeling of warmth and care among family members, or where emotional energy is focused; emotional energy in balanced families is distributed within the family and outside the family

- support -- emotional or other types of affirmation received by the family; balanced families welcome support from within as well as from outside

- decision-making -- balanced families can distinguish between decisions which involve all family members and decisions which are the primary or exclusive concern of an individual

- commonality -- time, space, interests, activities, and friends shared by family members; cohesive families emphasize family time and also encourage individual pursuits

Adaptability

Adaptability, from a family systems perspective, is the family's ability to change in response to situational and developmental stress. In strong families, adaptability reflects a balance between stability and change. Adaptable families show flexibility and stability when change occurs. A family's adaptability can be assessed by these indicators (Turnbull, Summers, & Brotherson, 1984):

- power structure -- the relative power and authority assigned to family members, a complex mixture of leadership, negotiation style, and allowed degrees of assertiveness; in balanced families, parents are in charge, yet children feel free to express opinions and negotiate

- role relationships -- who carries out tasks in the family; flexible families negotiate whatever role relationships best suit family members and meet family needs

- relationship rules -- clear rules and expectations guide the family's power structure and role relationships

Flexible families believe family members will act responsibly without a high degree of structure and control.

What special challenges to remaining flexible face families with handicapped children, where necessary routines are often a norm?

Communication

Communication is the process by which information is exchanged and transmitted in families and is considered the most important component of family dynamics. Open communication is important in establishing roles, expressing closeness or support, developing rules and expectations, and making family decisions. Open and honest communication has been characterized as the single most important factor affecting a person's well-being and relationships with others.

Effective communication involves sending clear messages, listening, and providing feedback. Communication in some families can be too closed -- highly intellectualized, unskilled, lacking focus on issues -- or too open -- heavily emotionalized, unskilled, permitting no private thoughts or feelings. Balanced families with positive communication skills discriminate between rational and emotional issues and also respect the right to private thoughts and feelings.

Understanding Family Interaction

Although family systems theory provides us with a philosophy and techniques which make working effectively with families increasingly likely, that does not mean that family interactions are simple, consistent, or easily evaluated. To the contrary, family interaction is a complex interplay among individuals and subsystems, where individuals have different roles within different subsystems.

Each family, as a unique entity, develops coping strategies that work for them. It is important not to judge or label a family. The majority of families with a handicapped child have arrived at a process which works for them and with which they are comfortable.

Family systems theory provides a useful framework for viewing the family as a whole. Skills, such as those employed by the effective help-giver, are discussed more thoroughly in upcoming sections of this manual. This combination of perspective and skills can lead to positive help-seeker/help-giver interactions and the successful completion and implementation of the IFSP.

Good communication skills are the most critical component of positive family interaction. It is also true that not all communication is verbal.

What are some of the different ways you can encourage good family communication skills in order to promote positive family interactions?

A Social Systems Perspective

Just as it is most effective to consider the whole family -- and not only the disabled child --when conducting assessments and planning interventions, it is also of great value to the family to consider them as a member of a larger network when assessing their strengths and capabilities.

When talking about focusing on the family in this training program, we will generally mean the family as it interacts, changes, develops, and achieves as a social unit embedded within other social units and connected to other social networks. This social systems perspective takes into account the effects that changes within one social unit can have on another social unit. In other words, related social units are seen as interdependent, just as family members are seen as interdependent.

Many of the social units in the family's wider social system are considered to be informal -- friends, family, co-workers, etc. -- while others are clearly formal in nature -- social service agencies, day care centers, physicians. Informal social support networks are critical to a family's development of its abilities to become self-sustaining because these sources of support are more readily available to families over time and because the support can be reciprocated.

To the extent that exchanges and events occurring between the family and these other social networks have a positive influence on the family and its functioning, they are considered to be supportive and health-promoting.

These relationships and exchanges provide the basis of a social systems definition of intervention which we will use in the course of this training and which is: **The provision of support (i.e., resources provided by others, whether material or educational resources, time, or emotional support) by members of a family's informal and formal social network that either directly or indirectly influences child, parent, and family functioning.**

Bronfenbrenner (1979) had these words to say about parenting tasks as viewed from a social systems perspective.

"Whether parents can perform effectively in their child-rearing roles depends on the *role demands, stresses, and supports emanating from other settings* [italics added] ... . Parents' evaluations of their own capacity to function, as well as their view of their child, are related to such external factors as *flexibility of job schedules, adequacy of child care arrangements, the presence of friends and neighbors who can help out in large and small emergencies* [italics added], the quality of health and social services, and neighborhood safety. The availability of supportive settings is, in turn, a function of their existence and frequency in a given culture or subculture. This frequency can be enhanced by the adoption of public policies and practices that create additional settings and societal roles conducive to family life"(p.7).

Why is the existence of informal support networks so important to a family experiencing great need?

Won't social agencies serve the same purpose?

The question now becomes, "How can we bring together the notions of an enabling model of helping families who are viewed from a social systems perspective in order to achieve the goal of promoting positive family functioning through the use of successfully written and implemented Family Support Plans?"

Perhaps the question itself seems a bit much at this time. Actually, you will spend the remainder of this training reading about and practicing the very skills which will demonstrate the answer to this question much better than a simple paragraph or two could presume to do. So, let's hold that question for now and instead, starting on the next page, summarize the principles upon which our model of family assessment and intervention is based. We have already stated that we wish to :

- **ENABLE FAMILIES.** When we speak of enabling families, we mean <u>creating opportunities and providing support</u> for the family or for individual family members to become more competent and independent in their efforts to meet their own needs and achieve their own goals.

- **EMPOWER FAMILIES.** The empowerment of families occurs as a result of carrying out family interventions in such a way that the family members experience a sense of <u>increased control over their lives</u> as the result of their own efforts and successes.

- **STRENGTHEN FAMILIES.** We can support families by helping them to <u>identify the things they already do well</u> (existing strengths) and encouraging them to use these capabilities to meet their present needs and achieve future goals.

- **STRENGTHEN FAMILY TIES TO INFORMAL SUPPORT NETWORKS.** Family <u>ties to and reliance on informal support networks should not be supplanted by professional services.</u> Strong relationships between the family and these support sources give the family greater control over their own lives, since this is support the family can access as needed. This kind of support can be reciprocal.

- **ENCOURAGE THE DEVELOPMENT OF NEW SKILLS AND COMPETENCIES.** Promoting the family's development of a wide variety of skills and competencies means <u>providing the family with the information, direction, and encouragement necessary to develop new strengths</u> and in turn become even more independent, more self-reliant.

Assessment and Intervention Guidelines

We now have an understanding of the direction we'd like to proceed in as we become more specific in defining our model for assessment and intervention. This is probably a good time for a reminder, too, that the purpose of this section of the training is to familiarize you with these principles, or guidelines, on which our model is based.

The purpose of the upcoming sections in this manual is to give you additional information and opportunities for practice. These will aid in transforming this from a paper and pencil process into a repertoire of tools which can be readily used by the skillful and informed practitioner working to support positive family functioning.

Below, then, is a list of the guidelines for working with families that are considered critical to the successful development of improved and positive family functioning. More detailed instruction for the help-giver can be found in the next four sections of this module.

Base intervention efforts on needs and aspirations identified by the family.

Rationale: The family must be willing to put its own time and energy into an effort that is to realize lasting change and improvement. This is much more likely to occur if the family personally identifies the needs and selects the projects on which to work. The role of the help-giver in this effort is to assist the family in identifying and prioritizing its needs.

Promote the use of existing strengths and capabilities to meet family needs.

Rationale: All families have certain strengths and capabilities, even though they may not recognize them as such. When the family's own abilities are used to obtain needed resources or to find solutions to problems, the family's confidence and self-esteem are enhanced. This success provides the encouragement for families to continue or increase their efforts to become independent and more self-reliant.

The role of the help-giver in this effort is to work with the family in identifying their strengths and to make whatever reasonable efforts are necessary to help the family utilize these capabilities.

Emphasize the importance of developing and maintaining strong family ties to informal support sources.

Rationale: Strong, working relationships between the family and members of its informal social network are critical to the development and well-being of a healthy family unit. Informal support is usually more readily available to families and can be more easily reciprocated, both of which can prevent the loss of self-esteem.

The help-giver must work with the family to identify all potential sources of informal support and be careful not to replace this informal support with formal/professional systems.

Expand and develop the family's repertoire of skills and competencies.

Rationale: While most families are not completely self-sustaining, families in great need may be considerably lacking in the skills and capabilities necessary to meet their own needs.

It is the help-giver's responsibility to employ helping behaviors which will create opportunities for the family's development of a wide variety of valuable skills and competencies. This in turn should promote interdependence, self-reliance, and increased self-esteem.

Wouldn't it be easier for you as a help-giver to simply solve some of the family's problems you've seen countless times before?

Why bother to enable, empower, strengthen, and encourage the development of families?

Family-Level Assessment and Intervention Model

Based on the preceding discussion, it now seems apparent that this model for assessment of and intervention with the family must include:

1. SPECIFICATION AND PRIORITIZATION OF FAMILY NEEDS AND ASPIRATIONS,

2. UTILIZATION OF EXISTING FAMILY STRENGTHS AND CAPABILITIES,

3. IDENTIFICATION OF SOURCES OF SUPPORT AND RESOURCES (ESPECIALLY INFORMAL) FOR MEETING NEEDS AND ACHIEVING ASPIRATIONS, AND

4. CREATION OF OPPORTUNITIES FOR THE DEVELOPMENT OF ADDITIONAL SKILLS AND COMPETENCIES.

While advancing through the upcoming sections of this module, you will be introduced to activities which will enhance professional skills used during interactions with the family and when developing IFSP's.

The next four sections of this training manual are listed on the following table. They refer to the principles of the model just stated and implementation of the model. After reading the section **Working With Families**, proceed to **Needs & Aspirations**, a critical component of the helping model.

Family-Level Assessment & Intervention Principles

SECTION	ASSESSMENT/INTERVENTION PRINCIPLE	IMPLEMENTATION
Needs & Aspirations	SPECIFICATION AND PRIORITIZATION OF FAMILY NEEDS AND ASPIRATIONS	Use needs-based assessment strategies and interviews to identify the needs and goals the family is willing to devote time and energy toward meeting and achieving.
Strengths & Capabilities	UTILIZATION OF EXISTING FAMILY STRENGTHS AND CAPABILITIES	Identify existing family strengths and skills which can be applied to meet present needs, as well as strengths which need to be developed to increase independence and self-reliance.
Support & Resources	IDENTIFICATION OF SOURCES OF SUPPORT AND RESOURCES FOR MEETING NEEDS AND ACHIEVING ASPIRATIONS	Use the procedure of "mapping" to identify both existing and potential sources of support and resources from among the family's personal social network.
The Effective Help-Giver	CREATION OF OPPORTUNITIES FOR THE DEVELOPMENT OF ADDITIONAL SKILLS AND COMPETENCIES	Employ helping behaviors and strategies which create opportunities for the family to develop a wide variety of abilities to be used to meet needs and achieve desired goals.

The figure to the right is one you will find at the beginning of each of the next four sections of the manual. It represents a system of gears, all of which influence and are influenced by one another.

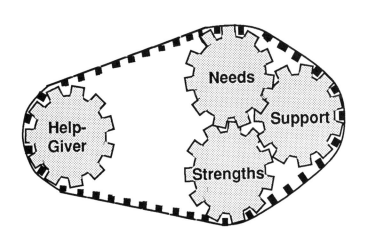

This is one useful way to picture the relationship between the family, as represented by the three gears to the right, and the help-giver.

The role of the help-giver is truly key to the ability of the family to realize its healthy potential.

Tips From the Text

Families do not exist in a vacuum but influence and are influenced by other formal and informal social units they come into contact with. To the extent that exchanges and events occurring between the family and these other social networks have a positive influence on the family and its functioning, they are considered to be supportive and health-promoting.

Since influences will always be there, it makes sense for the help-giver to work with the family in strengthening ties to those who are in a position to offer support and resources to the family in need.

Below is a statement of the key principles upon which our assessment and intervention model is based. Note that they are presented from the viewpoint of the help-giver, but imply time and effort on the part of the family.

1. ENABLE FAMILIES
2. EMPOWER FAMILIES
3. STRENGTHEN FAMILIES
4. STRENGTHEN FAMILY TIES TO INFORMAL SUPPORT NETWORKS
5. ENCOURAGE THE DEVELOPMENT OF NEW SKILLS AND COMPETENCIES

Guidelines for working with families in a way that promotes positive family functioning are summarized below. These guidelines will be presented in much greater detail in subsequent sections of this training manual.

- BASE INTERVENTION EFFORTS ON NEEDS AND ASPIRATIONS IDENTIFIED BY THE FAMILY.
- PROMOTE THE USE OF EXISTING STRENGTHS AND CAPABILITIES TO MEET FAMILY NEEDS.
- EMPHASIZE THE IMPORTANCE OF DEVELOPING AND MAINTAINING STRONG FAMILY TIES TO INFORMAL SUPPORT SOURCES.
- EXPAND AND DEVELOP THE FAMILY'S REPERTOIRE OF SKILLS AND COMPETENCIES.

Needs & Aspirations

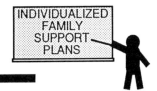

Trainer's Notes

Needs & Aspirations is the first of four sections which expand upon the principles presented in the last section, **Working with Families.** Following **Needs & Aspirations** will be sections on **Strengths & Capabilities, Support & Resources,** and **The Effective Help-Giver.**

Time

For a training group of 10 people, allow 2 hours to discuss this section, answer questions, and complete any exercises or activities.

Materials

For this session you will need:

- training manual for *Developing Individualized Family Support Plans*
- *Enabling and Empowering Families* (Dunst, Trivette & Deal, 1988)
- chalkboard and chalk or newsprint and markers, along with masking tape to attach pieces of newsprint to the wall
- optional: overhead transparencies
- optional: overhead projector and screen or light-colored wall

Before You Begin

- Be sure all equipment is set up properly.
- Read the material covered in the Training Manual on **Needs and Aspirations.**
- Complete the activities so you can answer questions about them.
- Be prepared to discuss the questions below.

Discussion Questions

❑ The model presented here for working with families requires that needs identified within the helping relationship be prioritized by the family. *How will this approach change your methods for working with families who are seeking help?*

❑ Try to think of specific examples or situations a family might present when it would be more appropriate to use a term other than "need" to describe an activity or project to which the family would be willing to devote time and energy. *What are some other terms that can be subsumed under the umbrella term "need"?*

❑ Needs can be placed along a continuum from the most basic to the most self-fulfilling and also grouped into categories which may have related solutions or which may influence one another. *How will ordering and grouping needs help you and the family as you work together?*

❑ A wealth of information can be obtained by meeting with the family to conduct a needs assessment interview. While the practiced interviewer will already have many skills at his/her disposal for this effort, the approach presented here can enhance the outcome of the assessment interview. *How can you begin immediately to take advantage of the guidelines for conducting interviews presented in this section of the training?*

Tips for Leading Discussion

- Ask if there are any questions from the first part of the reading.

- Anticipate trainee questions about managing the assessment interview. Are they concerned about the interview getting out of hand? Are they concerned that needs of the child will be overlooked if the family has too many other problems? What are other concerns?

- Try to get other trainees to respond to these concerns from their own experiences. Encourage trainees who have used this model for needs identification to share their experiences with the others. Remind trainees that when the family identifies a need which requires addressing, they must also commit <u>themselves</u> to that process.

- If trainees' experiences have not been positive, or if they lack experience in family-directed encounters, be sure to reinforce the attitudes and recommendations in these readings.

- Ask if there are any questions from the Interview Procedures part of the reading.

- Ask trainees if they have any additional suggestions for conducting interviews that are consistent with the social and family systems approach to assessment and intervention presented here.

Activities

There are two activities in this section. The second requires familiarity with the Family Needs Scale but not its completion during training.

Preparation for all activities

Complete both activities ahead of time; be prepared to answer questions about the Family Needs Scale.

Activity: Needs, Wants, & Wishes

5 MINUTES EXPLAIN ACTIVITY AND ANSWER QUESTIONS
Trainees will use space in the training manual to enter their own needs, wants, and wishes as defined in the activity.

10 MINUTES HAVE TRAINEES COMPLETE ACTIVITY

15 MINUTES DISCUSSION
After trainees share some items on their lists, focus discussion on the emotional component of their responses, e.g., the importance of certain items and related feelings. Is this true for clients also?

TOTAL TIME: 30 MINUTES

Activity: Family Needs Scale

5 MINUTES EXPLAIN ACTIVITY
Trainees will read the form (not complete it) and make notes about their responses to the questions.

5 MINUTES HAVE TRAINEES READ FORM THOROUGHLY
Ask for questions about the form or accompanying instructions.

15 MINUTES HAVE TRAINEES ANSWER QUESTIONS
Encourage trainees to formulate specific responses, whether written out completely or in note form.

15 MINUTES DISCUSS RESPONSES TO QUESTIONS
Emphasize the form as a tool to accompany a personal interview. Why would the form not give a "complete picture" of the family?

TOTAL TIME: 40 MINUTES

Points to Look For

In the previous section we discussed principles derived from social and family systems theory which form the basis of a model for effective assessment and intervention strategies. Use of this family-level intervention model increases the likelihood of positive outcomes for the family as a unit and for the child whose handicap brought the family into the service system.

The four principles stated suggest that family-level assessment and intervention include:

♦ 1. **Specification and prioritization of family needs and aspirations**

   2. Utilization of existing family strengths and capabilities

   3. Identification of sources of support and resources for meeting needs and achieving aspirations

   4. Effective help-giver roles in creating opportunities for the development of additional skills and competencies

In this section we will focus on the first of these principles -- family needs and aspirations. Below are listed some important points to look for and remember as you read. You can use the back of this page to make your own notes or responses to the items below.

Discussion Questions

❑ The model presented here for working with families requires that needs identified within the helping relationship be prioritized by the family. *How will this approach change your methods for working with families seeking help?*

❑ Try to think of specific examples or situations a family might present when it would be more appropriate to use a term other than "need" to describe an activity or project to which the family would be willing to devote time and energy. *What are some other terms that can be subsumed under the umbrella term "need"?*

❑ Needs can be placed along a continuum from the most basic to the most self-fulfilling and also grouped into categories which may have related solutions or which may influence one another. *How will ordering and grouping needs help you and the family as you work together?*

❑ A wealth of information can be obtained by meeting with the family to conduct a needs assessment interview. While the practiced interviewer will already have many skills at his/her disposal for this effort, the approach presented here can enhance the outcome of the assessment interview. *How can you begin immediately to take advantage of the guidelines for conducting interviews presented in this section of the training?*

Notes

NEEDS & ASPIRATIONS

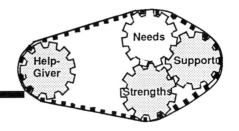

Research and observations on work with families of pre-school age children have repeatedly demonstrated that unmet needs may not only have negative effects on the health and well-being of the family, but may also increase the chances that professionally prescribed child-level interventions will be sacrificed because time, energy, and resources must be devoted elsewhere.

Therefore, failure of a family to subscribe to professional regimens may not indicate laziness, resistance, or an unwillingness to cooperate, but the existence of circumstances which draw the family's energy and efforts in other directions.

What Are Needs?

The American Heritage Dictionary defines "need" as *a condition or situation in which something necessary or desirable is required or wanted ... a wish for something that is lacking or desired ... something required or wanted; a requisite.*

Operationally, we can define "need" as the discrepancy between the help-seeker's assessment of his/her actual situation and the desired situation. Also, there is usually a sense of urgency or importance attending a need, as well as a willingness on the family's part to devote energy and resources to finding the resources to meet the need.

For the purpose of working with families to help them identify and prioritize their needs, it is useful for us to look even more closely at the attributes which must be present in order for need identification to occur. Each of these characteristics, or attributes, is presented from the viewpoint of the family or individual seeking help.

Specific Attributes of Needs

- **PSYCHOLOGICAL AWARENESS.** There must be an awareness on the part of the family or individual that there is a problem, that something is missing, that things are not as they ought to be. Only if a condition is different enough or unpleasant enough in the eyes of the family will there be an effort to alleviate or reduce the discrepancy.

If the help-giver defines a need that the family does not recognize, then the need does not exist for the family. For example, the help-giver may believe there is a need for a child to be in a day care center. If the family does not have the same expectation and does not consider this a priority, then for them there is no need.

- **VALUE INFLUENCE.** Not only must the reality of a situation or the recognition of a discrepancy be considered when defining a need or problem, but equally important is the family's judgment that this discrepancy or absence of something desired will influence or already is influencing their behavior. This is value influence.

An extreme example of this situation could occur with the death of one of the parents in a given family. Although the difference between what the family was accustomed to ("ought to be") and the reality of their present situation is undeniable, the family may not judge the loss as one which will significantly influence their behavior, especially if there are financial and emotional resources to support them through a difficult time. In other words, the family does not turn immediately to looking for a replacement for the lost spouse/parent.

On the other hand, a family's judgment of a need which they believe is having an effect on their well-being or healthy functioning must be taken seriously, even when the effect does not seem apparent to the help-giver. As Thomas and Thomas noted some sixty years ago, *"If (people) define situations as real, they are real in their consequences"* (p.572).

- **NEED RECOGNITION.** Need recognition is the desire for whatever it may be that will reduce or resolve a need. In order for this desire to be present, of course, there must be an awareness -- or at least a notion on the part of the help-seeker -- that the resource for meeting the need exists.

A family with a handicapped child may exhaust themselves trying to provide all the care and nurture for the child if they have no idea that there are educational and community resources available to assist in this effort. If the family believes that what is being done by them is all that can possibly be done for their child, they may not consider themselves as being in need.

- **SOLUTION IDENTIFICATION.** Finally, we should also remember that families may have needs they no longer call needs -- even if they realize that there is something they are lacking, that the absence of this condition or thing is affecting their lives, and that there are resources to meet their needs -- <u>if</u> they perceive themselves as having absolutely no way of obtaining those resources to meet the needs.

The experience of one agency staff person illustrates the necessity of solution identification. This individual from the agency -- call him Sam -- arrived at the home of a family for an initial interview on a rainy day. Upon entering the house, Sam noticed two things: first, that water was literally pouring into the house through a hole in the roof, and second, that the family seemed oblivious to this situation.

Sam chose not to comment on this condition at first, but went about explaining his agency and its services and establishing rapport with the family. Later during the conversation, as things were proceeding well, Sam asked how the hole had come in the roof.

The family readily explained that they had rented the only house they could afford, couldn't get the landlord to fix the hole in the roof, couldn't get the landlord to buy the materials so they could fix the hole in the roof, and couldn't afford the materials themselves to fix the hole on the roof. The family told Sam that they had just decided to live with the problem because they could not see any way to secure the resources necessary to remedy their situation. It is apparent the family no longer considered their condition to be one of need, because they had exhausted all possible solutions to the problem.

Your ability to recognize and keep in mind these four attributes which substantially influence the needs identification process will serve you well in your work with families. Let's summarize them before moving on:

1. Psychological Awareness
2. Value Influence   *I need*
3. Need Recognition
4. Solution Identification

> *Have you worked with families who didn't identify needs you thought existed?*
>
> *Based on what you've just read, why might that have happened?*

Needs ... and More Needs

You've probably noticed by now that there are a number of terms we use more or less interchangeably with the word "need." Since we have decided that the term "need" can refer to any urgent or important condition or situation to which a family is willing to devote time, energy and resources in order to reduce the discrepancy between "what is" and "what is desired," it is not difficult to think of other terms which also fit that description. In this training module, we will often refer to "needs, desires, aspirations, and goals" when we describe a family's situation which fits the conditions stated above. Other appropriate terms include "aims, wants, wishes, projects, priorities, and ambitions." Can you think of any others?

Stop and Practice Your Skills

Activity: Needs, Wants, & Wishes

Even though there are many terms which will be used interchangeably for the term "need," there are times when use of these alternate terms is deliberate and should be recognized as such. For instance, used correctly, the terms "needs, wants, and wishes" denote different degrees of desire and necessity. Consider this as you complete the exercise below, and remain aware of the distinctions as you work with families to identify needs, and at the same time dignify wants and wishes.

would be
a good
activity!

 Consider your life situation now and use the space on the facing page below the column headings to list your responses to these questions.

- What are things you truly <u>need</u> now?
- What are things you don't really need, but <u>want</u> very much?
- What are things you <u>wish</u> for, though you believe you will probably never have?

Discuss your responses with other group members in terms of:

1. the importance you feel for your responses, regardless of their practicality or necessity
2. emotional issues related to your wants and wishes

Needs	Wants	Wishes

Needs vs. Concerns

Frequently, families will not directly express their needs, but will rather tell you about "concerns, worries, problems, difficulties, dilemmas, or/ uneasiness" they have. While this is a good starting point, there is work to be done before actual needs can be identified. As a help-giver, you must help the family translate their concerns or worries into clearly stated needs. Why?

Concerns (e.g., "Johnny's speech is not developing very well," "Mary's teacher says she's always tired at school") are conditions which make families aware of discrepancies between the way things are and the way they would like them to be; that something is not right and needs attention. Concerns let families and help-givers define conditions or situations the family does not want to continue. Concerns, however, √ do not provide information about what resources are needed to rectify the discrepant situation.

Need recognition, on the other hand, involves the identification of resources which will reduce or resolve the expressed need. As a help-giver, you will frequently have to take concerns presented to you and assist the family in clarifying or distilling these concerns in such a way that "what the family does not want" becomes "what the family needs," so that resources can be identified to fill that need.

The relationship between concerns and needs is expressed like this:

- Concerns are conditions that lead to a recognition that the difference between "what is" and "what is desired" is marked enough to warrant attention.
- Needs are conditions that lead to the recognition that "something" will reduce the discrepancy between "what is" and "what is desired".
- Concerns reveal discrepancies; needs identification (recognition) begins the process of reducing discrepancies.

Ordering and Grouping Needs

Most of us would agree that some needs (e.g., food, shelter) are more critical than others, yet at the same time we must also recognize and respect the individual differences among families when it comes to the creation of their own needs hierarchies. Family needs and needs hierarchies are often very distinct and highly personalized. They must be identified and prioritized from the family's and not the help-giver's perspective if it is the family who are to provide the effort to meet these needs.

After a discussion of needs hierarchies and categories of needs, we will review methods and techniques you can employ to help identify those needs which are unique and personal to an individual family.

Needs Hierarchies

One hierarchy of needs which is familiar to many of us is that which was developed by Abraham Maslow and first published in 1954. According to Maslow, needs can be placed along a continuum -- usually represented in pyramid form rather than linearly -- from the most basic to the most highly specialized, the need to realize one's true potential in life.

Maslow's Hierarchy of Needs

*self-actualization

*realizing one's potential - being able to do what you enjoy doing and do well

esteem needs
(success, self-respect)

belonging, love needs
(affection, affiliation, identification)

safety needs
(security, stability, order)

(basic) physiological needs
(hunger, thirst, sex)

This order from "lowest to highest" also represents the order in which needs must be met, according to Maslow. A person concerned with basic physiological needs such as hunger and thirst will not have the energy to devote to higher level needs such as a steady job, meaningful relationships, or personal and professional success until basic needs are met. In other words, unmet basic needs will dominate an individual's behavior and interfere with achievement of higher-level needs.

The term "environmental press" can also be used to refer to the way in which needs influence behavior. Garbarino (1982, p. 13) defined environmental press as

> "... the combined influence of forces working in an environment to shape the behavior and development of individuals in that setting. It arises from the circumstances confronting and surrounding an individual that generate (needs and) psychosocial momentum, which *tend to guide the individual in a particular direction*" (italics added).

This suggests that the strongest forces or conditions (needs) in an individual's (or family's) environment will take precedence over competing forces (needs) to steer behavior a particular direction. This is consistent with our premise that those needs identified by the family as being most necessary to be met will be those which influence family behavior in the direction of committing time, energy, and resources to resolve. And, it is likewise consistent with Maslow's contention that basic needs must be met first; Maslow just goes a step further to describe which needs are the most basic.

Needs Categories

Besides organizing needs in hierarchies, it is also possible to group them into categories. Familiarize yourself with these categories and examples or keep a list nearby to help you structure your efforts to assist the family in identifying needs.

Needs Categories and Needs

FINANCES	FOOD/CLOTHING/SHELTER	HEALTH/PROTECTION
• money for necessities • money for special needs • money for the future • a steady job • learning to budget	• adequate and balanced diet • good drinking water • enough clean/decent clothes for each season • clean environment • adequate housing and furniture • heat/water/electricity • safe neighborhoods	• availability of routine health and dental care • availability of emergency health and dental care • confidence in health care professionals • availability of legal protection • adequate public safety protection

---

(Continued on next page.)

VOCATION

- opportunity to work
- satisfaction with work (in or outside the home)
- job security

RECREATION

- availability of recreational activities for children, parents, whole family
- opportunities to take advantage of recreation

CHILD CARE

- help with routine child care
- emergency child care
- availability of day care/ baby-sitting

COMMUNICATION/ TRANSPORTATION

- means of contacting family, friends, etc.
- access to a telephone
- availability of safe/ adequate transportation

ADULT EDUCATION/ENRICHMENT

- availability of adult education opportunities
- access to educational opportunities
- resources for self-education/enrichment

CHILD EDUCATION/ENRICHMENT

- child educational opportunities
- availability of/access to special intervention services
- opportunities to play with other children
- access to integrated community experiences

EMOTIONAL SUPPORT

- positive intrafamily relationships
- positive relationships outside the family
- companionship
- sense of belonging to family or other group
- opportunities to spend time with significant others
- availability of time for one's self

CULTURAL/SOCIAL OPPORTUNITIES

- opportunities for ethnic or value-related experiences with others
- opportunities for involvement in cultural/community affairs
- opportunities for involvement in social activities

OTHER

Think About It...

> Can you think of additional categories to add?
>
> Can you think of items to list under "other" or beneath existing categories?

The Effect of Needs on Family Functioning

Several studies conducted at the Family, Infant & Preschool Program in Morganton, North Carolina, have revealed the extent to which unmet needs affect individual and family functioning and interfere with professionally prescribed regimens for infants and preschoolers whose families were clients of the program (see accompanying text, p.20).

All families in the studies completed instruments which assessed needs and adequacy of resources. Parents also completed well-being measures that assessed both their physical and emotional health. Finally, in two of the three studies, parents were asked to indicate the extent to which they had time, energy, and personal commitment to carry out child-level educational and therapeutic interventions.

The results of the studies can be succinctly summarized:

- The greater the number of unmet needs, the greater the number of emotional and physical problems reported by the parents.

- The greater the number of needs unrelated to child-level interventions, the greater the probability that parents revealed they did not have the time, energy, or personal investment to carry out interventions prescribed for their child.

Implications for Work with Families

What are the implications for our work with families, based on the knowledge we now have regarding needs, needs hierarchies, and the effects of unmet needs on family functioning? At least two major implications present themselves:

1. First, the relationships among family resources, well-being, and professionally recommended child-level interventions indicate that before parents are asked to carry out these interventions, efforts to help the family meet their other needs -- which they consider a higher priority -- should be made. Only then will parents have the time and energy to work with their children to achieve educational and therapeutic goals.

2. Second, if parents are expected to function in an educational or therapeutic capacity with their children when they have other more pressing needs, these added demands can result in a number of unhealthy consequences. These may include stress, negative feelings toward the child, and a breakdown of the relationship among family members.

The available data clearly indicate a need to adopt a family-level, social systems approach to early intervention practices in order to truly respond and be responsible to the ever-evolving needs of families.

Family Needs Checklist

What Are Needs?

☐ The term "need" means any perception of importance or urgency that results in a family allocating time, energy, and resources to reduce the discrepancy between *what is* and *what is desired or ought to be*.

☐ Besides "need," other terms which fit the definition above include: desires, goals, aspirations, wants, wishes, projects, aims, priorities, and ambitions.

☐ The terms "needs, wants, and wishes" are used interchangeably in many situations, yet used correctly they denote different degrees of desire and necessity.

Specific Attributes of Needs

☐ <u>Psychological Awareness</u>: a concern or perception that there is a difference between the way things are and the way things ought or are desired to be.

☐ <u>Value Influence</u>: a personal judgment that the (real/perceived) difference between what is and what is desired will influence or is influencing behavior.

☐ <u>Need Recognition</u>: an awareness that there does exist a resource which will reduce the discrepancy between what is and what is desired/ought to be.

☐ <u>Solution Identification</u>: the belief that there is some way to obtain the necessary resource to meet the existing need.

Needs vs. Concerns

☐ Concerns are conditions that lead to a recognition that the difference between what is and what is desired is marked enough to warrant attention.

☐ Needs are conditions that lead to the recognition that "something" will reduce the discrepancy between what is and what is desired.

☐ Concerns reveal discrepancies; identifying and acknowledging needs begins the process of reducing discrepancies.

Ordering and Grouping Needs

☐ Needs should be identified and prioritized by the family, with the assistance of the professional help-giver. Identification of family-prioritized -- not professionally-prioritized -- needs should be the goal of the needs-based assessment.

☐ Needs hierarchies are ways of ordering needs from the most basic to the most highly specialized.

☐ Unmet basic needs will dominate an individual's or family's behavior and interfere with achievement of higher-level needs; therefore, those needs identified by the family as being most necessary to be met will be those which influence family behavior in the direction of committing time, energy, and resources to resolve.

☐ Categorizing needs will assist you, the help-giver, structure your efforts to assist the family in identifying and prioritizing their needs.

The Effect of Needs on Family Functioning

☐ The greater the number of unmet family needs, the greater the number of emotional and physical problems reported in surveys by parents.

☐ The greater the number of family needs unrelated to child-level interventions, the greater the probability that parents will not have the time, energy, or personal investment to carry out interventions prescribed for their child.

☐ Expecting parents to function in an educational or therapeutic capacity with their child when they have other more pressing needs creates added demands that are likely to result in any number of unhealthy consequences. These consequences may include stress, negative feelings toward the child, or a breakdown of the relationship between the family and the help-giver.

☐ Before parents are asked to carry out professionally prescribed regimens on behalf of their child, efforts to help the family meet other needs -- which they consider to be of a higher priority -- must be made.

Stop and Practice Your Skills

Activity: Family Needs Scale

On the next page is a copy of the Family Needs Scale which can be helpful for some families as they work to define their needs. After the family completes the scale (which really pinpoints concerns), use their responses as discussion starting points. Encourage them to describe more fully the conditions that influenced them in assessing their situation, as you work to help clarify their needs more precisely.

Because of the specificity of the content, it would probably not be useful for you to complete this scale for yourself. Do look it over carefully, though, and discuss the questions below with other members of your group or some of your colleagues.

Questions

    A. How would you introduce and present this scale to a family for completion? What words would you use to clearly, and in a non-threatening way, explain the purpose of the scale?

    B. How would you begin a discussion with the family based on their responses?

    C. This approach to working with families is based on family-identified needs. If there were needs you expected to find rated "high" on the scale by the family, but which were not, how would you handle the situation?

    D. Would you use this scale with all families? Why or why not?

Family Needs Scale

Carl J. Dunst, Carolyn S. Cooper, Janet C. Weeldreyer, Kathy D. Snyder, and Joyce H. Chase

Name_____ Date_____

This scale asks you to indicate if you have a need for any type of help or assistance in 41 different areas. Please *circle* the response that best describes how you feel about needing help in those areas.

To what extent do you feel the need for any of the following types of help or assistance:	Not Applicable	Almost Never	Seldom	Sometimes	Often	Almost Always
1. Having money to buy necessities and pay bills	NA	1	2	3	4	5
2. Budgeting money	NA	1	2	3	4	5
3. Paying for special needs of my child	NA	1	2	3	4	5
4. Saving money for the future	NA	1	2	3	4	5
5. Having clean water to drink	NA	1	2	3	4	5
6. Having food for two meals for my family	NA	1	2	3	4	5
7. Having time to cook healthy meals for my family	NA	1	2	3	4	5
8. Feeding my child	NA	1	2	3	4	5
9. Getting a place to live	NA	1	2	3	4	5
10. Having plumbing, lighting, heat	NA	1	2	3	4	5
11. Getting furniture, clothes, toys	NA	1	2	3	4	5
12. Completing chores, repairs, home improvements	NA	1	2	3	4	5
13. Adapting my house for my child	NA	1	2	3	4	5
14. Getting a job	NA	1	2	3	4	5
15. Having a satisfying job	NA	1	2	3	4	5
16. Planning for future job of my child	NA	1	2	3	4	5
17. Getting where I need to go	NA	1	2	3	4	5
18. Getting in touch with people I need to talk to	NA	1	2	3	4	5
19. Transporting my child	NA	1	2	3	4	5
20. Having special travel equipment for my child	NA	1	2	3	4	5
21. Finding someone to talk to about my child	NA	1	2	3	4	5
22. Having someone to talk to	NA	1	2	3	4	5
23. Having medical and dental care for my family	NA	1	2	3	4	5
24. Having time to take care of myself	NA	1	2	3	4	5
25. Having emergency health care	NA	1	2	3	4	5
26. Finding special dental and medical care for my child	NA	1	2	3	4	5
27. Planning for future health needs	NA	1	2	3	4	5
28. Managing the daily needs of my child at home	NA	1	2	3	4	5
29. Caring for my child during work hours	NA	1	2	3	4	5
30. Having emergency child care	NA	1	2	3	4	5
31. Getting respite care for my child	NA	1	2	3	4	5
32. Finding care for my child in the future	NA	1	2	3	4	5
33. Finding a school placement for my child	NA	1	2	3	4	5
34. Getting equipment or therapy for my child	NA	1	2	3	4	5
35. Having time to take my child to appointments	NA	1	2	3	4	5
36. Exploring future educational options for my child	NA	1	2	3	4	5
37. Expanding my education, skills, and interests	NA	1	2	3	4	5
38. Doing things that I enjoy	NA	1	2	3	4	5
39. Doing things with my family	NA	1	2	3	4	5
40. Participation in parent groups or clubs	NA	1	2	3	4	5
41. Traveling/vacationing with my child	NA	1	2	3	4	5

Source: C.J. Dunst, C.M. Trivette, and A.G. Deal (1988). *Enabling and Empowering Families: Principles and Guidelines for Practice*. Cambridge, MA: Brookline Books. May be reproduced.

Methods for Identifying Needs

The most effective method for identifying family needs is by face-to-face interview, since only in this way can the help-giver clarify any misunderstandings and explore fully family concerns and priorities. The use of assessment scales, such as the Family Needs Scale just presented, can sometimes supplement information obtained during an interview. Both approaches are designed to engage the family in identifying what they consider their needs, wants, goals, and aspirations. **It cannot be emphasized too strongly that identification and prioritization of needs by the family, and not by the help-giver, are the goals of the assessment process presented in this training.**

While it is often very difficult to do, professionals who can approach families without pre-conceived ideas of what needs to be done to improve their quality of life stand a much better chance of establishing a healthy and productive working relationship with the family. This type of working relationship, in turn, is conducive to family growth and independence. Stoneman (1985) stated this in the following way: *"To be effective [in work with families], service providers must want to hear what parents have to say and must be truly interested in understanding the family's concerns and needs"* (p.463).

The interview process we describe next is captured in the following exchange between a mother and a help-giver:

Mother: I worry every time anyone in the family gets sick.

Help-Giver: Can you tell me more about what worries you?

Mother: Well, it just costs so much money to see a doctor or a dentist or to buy medicine -- you see we don't have health insurance. Usually we don't get medical help when we need to because we don't have the money.

Help-Giver: I see. You're worried because when someone in the family needs a doctor, or a prescription, or some other kind of health care, you can't get it. You need money, or health insurance, or some way to get free medical care.

Mother: That's exactly right! We need a way to get medical treatment for illnesses that we can't treat ourselves.

What different needs might the mother in the scenario above have been trying to express with the beginning statement, "I worry every time anyone in the family gets sick"?

 **Interview Procedures**

At the time you are participating in this training you may have had relatively limited experience conducting family interviews or you may have spent a good deal of time doing just that. Practice and experience help you refine your style and streamline the process. Both the eager, new enthusiast and the seasoned veteran, however, can benefit from a set of guidelines for this complicated process, especially when new goals are introduced as we have done in this training.

Take the time to read through these guidelines thoroughly. During discussion, share with your group any additional guidelines you already use which are consistent with the family-level, needs-based model presented here. The guidelines are summarized in the checklist at the end of this discussion.

- **CLEARLY STATE THE REASON YOU'D LIKE TO VISIT WITH THE FAMILY WHEN SCHEDULING THE INTERVIEW.** For example, "I'd like to visit with your family next week so we can talk more about the needs and concerns you've told me about today."

- **ESTABLISH AN ATMOSPHERE DURING THE INITIAL CONTACT THAT IS ESPECIALLY POSITIVE, CLEAR, AND NON-THREATENING.** For example, "I'm really glad to have this chance to get to know all of you. I'll be as helpful as I can, but I need you and your family to <u>lead us</u> -- to <u>decide what the concerns are we'll work on and how you'd like to go about meeting your needs.</u>" *+ to set expectation*

  This approach makes clear early on what you expect your work together to accomplish (in a global sense), how you will contribute to this end, and what is expected of the family. Your straightforward, positive approach will mark a good beginning to the relationship-building process which will be crucial to the success of your efforts.

- **ENCOURAGE THE FAMILY TO INCLUDE ALL IMPORTANT FAMILY MEMBERS AND SIGNIFICANT OTHERS IN THE INTERVIEW.** For example, "I'd like to meet all the members of your family during my visit, Ms Jones and anyone else important to your family, like your fiancé. Will you ask them all to be there?"

  Complete, or nearly complete, family participation will allow you to observe patterns of interaction within the family and will present an excellent opportunity for you to get other perspectives on family needs and goals. Often, full family participation is not possible, however, and there will be times you will wish to meet with selected family members only. Remain flexible and take advantage of those present for the interview.

- **IF POSSIBLE, ARRANGE TO CONDUCT THE INTERVIEW IN A SETTING FAMILIAR TO THE FAMILY.** You will get a better picture of the family if they are in a familiar setting since they will likely be more relaxed and at ease. You can also use this opportunity to make your own assessment of the family's living situation.

- **START THE INTERVIEW BY FINDING OUT EACH PERSON'S NAME, ACKNOWLEDGING HIS OR HER PRESENCE, AND ESTABLISHING EACH PERSON'S RELATIONSHIP IN OR TO THE FAMILY.**

  Chat briefly with everyone present, including all children whose names you must also learn, and establish each person's relationship with the family. Thank each individual for being present, either directly or by acknowledging any extra effort put forth by the individual to attend. Show a genuine interest in the things each person shares with you; this information is often useful later on for involving family members in the interview. A good beginning helps put everyone at ease and increases the chances for a successful interview.

- **RESTATE FOR ALL PRESENT BOTH THE PURPOSE OF THE INTERVIEW AND WHAT YOU EXPECT TO ACCOMPLISH.** For example, "Emma told me about her concerns for the family when we spoke on the phone, so I do have some information. I'd like for all of you to tell me more about your family and your child's needs today so I can be as useful as possible in helping you find solutions to some of your needs."

  This is the family's meeting and this should be clear to all present. They will set the agenda in terms of identifying and prioritizing needs, usually with your help. Your job then is to put the family in control, while instilling in them a sense of confidence in you and establishing a partnership. This may take patience and practice on your part, but will certainly pay off in the end.

- **AS THE INTERVIEW GETS UNDER WAY, TRY TO GET THE "BIG PICTURE" BY LETTING EACH PERSON TELL HIS OR HER "STORY."** Listen and encourage participation -- but not useless rambling. Pay particular attention to the ways the family typically addresses its needs. Listen for aspirations and goals as well as concerns and problems.

- **KEEP A THOROUGH, RUNNING ACCOUNT OF THE NEEDS, CONCERNS, GOALS, AND ASPIRATIONS THAT THE FAMILY MEMBERS DESCRIBE DURING THE INTERVIEW.** Make written notes unless you're expert at committing a lot of new information to memory; you'll want to be sure that the needs the family does describe are subsequently addressed in more detail.

- **HELP THE FAMILY DETERMINE AND CLARIFY THE CONCERNS THAT ARE MOST IMPORTANT TO THEM OR MOST URGENT FROM THIS GENERAL DISCUSSION.** Concerns must be explored thoroughly and clarified until you and the family agree upon their specific nature. For instance, "I know you want your daughter to walk eventually, but I also hear you saying that it would be helpful if she could just get herself from room to room right now" calls for a different approach than does "I understand you are concerned about your daughter's chances of ever walking."

Use your skills as an active listener, reflect and paraphrase statements made by family members, and ask directly for clarification of complicated issues. A family may lack money, for example, due to unemployment, poor budgeting, very high medical bills, or any of a number of causes.

Knowing the factors that create and contribute to a difficult situation will guide you in the types of aid and assistance you present to the family to explore for meeting their needs. (NOTE: This process can frequently result in needs being redefined; be prepared to make adjustments when necessary so time is not wasted on ineffectual remedies.)

- **BE SENSITIVE AND RESPONSIVE TO VERBAL AND NONVERBAL MESSAGES CONVEYED BY ALL PRESENT, AND RESPOND AND REFLECT ON WHAT YOU SEE AND HEAR.** For example, "You say you want Bobby to be able to eat more independently, but I hear some hesitancy in your voice. Are you doubting the possibility of this happening?" Tone of voice, posture, uneasiness, and hesitations in speech are messages that you should acknowledge and clarify.

- **CONTINUE ACTIVE AND REFLECTIVE LISTENING THROUGHOUT THE INTERVIEW.** The most useful techniques are open-ended questions ("What are your ideas or feelings about ... ?"); leading statements ("Tell me more about ... ?"); and requests for clarification ("Do I understand you to be saying ... ?").

- **AFTER ESTABLISHING CONSENSUS AMONG FAMILY MEMBERS ABOUT THE NEEDS THEY IDENTIFY, CONCLUDE BY RESTATING THOSE NEEDS AND ESTABLISHING WITH THE FAMILY THE ORDER IN WHICH THEY SHOULD BE ADDRESSED.**

The ability to conduct an effective assessment interview requires time and practice; it is a skill that can be learned and perfected. Remember that your efforts at assisting a family identify resources and sources of support for meeting their true needs may be ineffective if the goals of the assessment interview are not successfully met.

Those who wish to improve their interviewing skills through further practice are referred to the volumes below which are accompanied by workbooks.

- Egan, G. (1986). *The skilled helper: A systematic approach to effective helping* (3rd edition). Pacific Grove, CA: Brooks/Cole Publishing Co.
- Carkhuff, R. R. (1987). *The art of helping vi* (6th edition). Amherst, MA: Human Resource Development Press, Inc.

The Effective Help-Giver

Clearly there is more to be said about successful interviewing procedures than has been presented in this section on **Needs & Aspirations**.

In the section of this training module entitled **The Effective Help-Giver** you will explore in greater detail the characteristics of successful help-giver/help-seeker exchanges -- rather than techniques for achieving specific goals. They are precisely the characteristics which should distinguish the assessment interview process and so are listed briefly below:

- establishing an effective working partnership with the family
- employing skills for effective communication
- being open, honest, and up-front with the family
- understanding family needs -- not every detail of the family's life
- focusing on solutions rather than causes and responsibility
- emphasizing action to meet needs rather than prolonged discussions of problems
- respecting the confidentiality of the help-giver/help-seeker relationship at all times.

Identifying Family Needs Checklist

Methods for Identifying Family Needs

☐ Use assessment tools like the face-to-face interview, the Family Needs Scale, or a combination of the two to help the family identify and prioritize their needs.

Interview Procedures

Be positive and take the lead in arranging the first interview with the family.

☐ When scheduling the interview, clearly state the purpose of your visit.

☐ Create a positive and non-threatening atmosphere for the interview by reassuring the family that your goal is to help them identify their needs and to help them find and take advantage of resources for meeting their needs.

☐ Encourage the family to invite all close family members and any significant others to participate in the interview.

☐ Arrange to conduct the interview in a setting familiar to the family, if at all possible.

Take time to establish rapport with the family and put them at ease before beginning the interview.

☐ Learn the name of each person present, including all children, and establish relationships with and within the family.

☐ Acknowledge each person's presence, especially by thanking him or her for being present for the interview.

☐ Briefly chat with each person, showing interest in what each has to share with you.

Begin by clearly stating the purpose of the interview.

☐ Restate the purpose of the visit and what you hope to accomplish for all present.

☐ Make it clear that this is the family's meeting to establish their agenda.

☐ Stress that you are there to learn about them, their needs, and their goals in order to be of as much help as possible.

Record both the aspirations and concerns of family members.

☐ Let the family just "tell its story."

☐ Pay attention to each member's concerns, aspirations, and statements about how the family typically addresses its needs.

☐ Make written or mental notes to be certain that any needs the family does describe can each be addressed in detail later on.

Help the family clarify concerns and define the precise nature of their needs.

☐ Clarify concerns by reflecting upon what is said, rephrasing statements, and asking for explanations or more detail.

☐ Try to get at the reasons for the family's needs: knowing why they lack a certain resource will help you guide them to the most appropriate sources of aid and assistance.

☐ Be prepared to redefine previously stated needs as you continue with the clarification process.

Be an empathic, responsive, and active listener throughout the interview.

☐ Be sensitive and responsive to verbal and non-verbal messages from all family members.

☐ Practice active listening by responding to and reflecting back what you hear.

☐ Use open-ended questions, leading statements, and requests for clarification to get information and demonstrate your concern.

Establish consensus regarding the priority needs, goals, etc.

☐ After reaching consensus with the family, restate the identified needs.

☐ Help the family achieve consensus in prioritizing these needs.

Strengths & Capabilities

Trainer's Notes

Strengths & Capabilities is the second of the four sections which expand upon the four principles presented in the section entitled: **Working with Families.** This section builds on the previous section, **Needs & Aspirations,** and will be followed by sections on **Support & Resources,** and **The Effective Help-Giver.**

Time

For a training group of 10 people, allow 3 hours to discuss this section, answer questions, and complete any exercises or activities.

Materials

For this session you will need to have:

- training manual for *Developing Individualized Family Support Plans*
- *Enabling and Empowering Families* (Dunst, Trivette & Deal, 1988)
- chalkboard and chalk or newsprint and markers, along with masking tape to attach pieces of newsprint to the wall
- optional: overhead transparencies of forms to be completed (Family Functioning Style Scale and Scoring Form)
- optional: overhead projector and screen or light-colored wall

Before You Begin

- Be certain that equipment and seating is prepared properly.
- Read the material in the manual on **Strengths and Capabilities.**
- Practice filling out the forms so that you can answer questions about them.
- Be prepared to discuss the questions (below).

 Discussion Questions

❑ When using the term "strengths," a help-giver should be careful not to imply the opposite--weaknesses. For this reason, the term "Family Functioning Style" is used to refer to a family's unique combination of strengths and capabilities. *How can you focus on strengths, while avoiding comparisons to weaknesses?*

❑ A family is a system of individuals possessing capabilities. A help-giver should look for these resources in individual family members and strong points in the interactions among family members. *What are some signs of strengths and capabilities in a family?*

❑ Focusing on the family's good points rather than only on problems makes the intervention more positive. *How can you adapt your approach to intervention in order to focus more on strengths?*

❑ If a family can build on their good points, they are more likely to feel successful in meeting needs. *How can you encourage this success?*

Tips for Leading Discussion

- Ask if there are any questions from the first part of the reading.

- Encourage trainees to talk about concerns they think they might have when allowing the family to direct the process of identification of strengths. Also discuss ways to phrase questions in order to elicit discussion of strengths.

- Try to get other trainees to respond to these concerns and issues from their own experiences.

- If trainees' experiences have not been positive, or if they lack experience in family-directed encounters, be sure to reinforce the attitudes and recommendations in these readings.

- Ask if there are any questions from the Interview Procedures part of the reading.

- You may want to discuss each part of the interview section and then follow with a "mini" role-play, where you have someone give an example of how they might use that procedure in an interview.

- Ask trainees if they have any additional suggestions for conducting interviews that are consistent with our social and family systems approach to assessment and intervention.

Activities

There are three activities in this section that involve filling out forms and learning how to use these forms in intervention settings. Use the following guidelines for these activities.

Preparation for all activities

You should be comfortable with the forms (fill them out ahead of time for practice) so that you can answer questions.

Activity: Family Strengths Grid

where

2 MINUTES   EXPLAIN EXERCISE
Trainees will use copies of grid included in the training manual and will fill the form out using their own families as the "clients."

3 MINUTES   HAVE TRAINEES READ INSTRUCTIONS AND QUESTIONS THOROUGHLY
Ask them if there are any questions on the instructions or the form itself.

10 MINUTES   HAVE TRAINEES FILL OUT GRID ON THEMSELVES
Trainees should fill out the form as if they were interviewing a family, but should use information from their own families instead.

10 MINUTES   DISCUSSION
Suggest that the trainees give a copy of the grid to their own family members, so that they can compare results. Discuss what might cause differences in the results.

TOTAL TIME: 25 MINUTES

Activity: Family Functioning Style Scale

5 MINUTES   EXPLAIN EXERCISE
Trainees will use copies of form included in the training manual and will fill the form out using their own families as the "clients."

5 MINUTES   HAVE TRAINEES READ FORM THOROUGHLY
Ask them if there are any questions on the instructions or the form itself.

20 MINUTES   HAVE TRAINEES FILL OUT FORM ON THEMSELVES
Trainees should fill out the form as if they were interviewing a family, but should use information from their own families instead.

15 MINUTES   DISCUSS FORM
How will you be able to use the form to identify family capabilities? Are there ways the form can be adapted to meet special needs, if necessary?

TOTAL TIME: 45 MINUTES

Alternate approach

Group trainees into pairs and have them interview each other in order to fill out the form. This will give the trainees experience in using the interviewing procedures, but will probably take more time than the approach described above.

If you choose this approach, follow steps 1, 2, and 4 above, but use the following as step 3 instead of step 3 above.

40 MINUTES   HAVE TRAINEES INTERVIEW PARTNER TO FILL OUT FORM
Trainees should use the interviewing procedures discussed in this section to interview their partners. They should use the information gained in the interview to fill out the form. Then, the partners should switch roles. Make sure the first interviewer does not take more than half the allotted time, so that the second interviewer is not rushed to finish in a short time.

TOTAL TIME FOR ALTERNATE APPROACH: 1 HOUR, 5 MINUTES

Activity: Scoring Form

5 MINUTES   EXPLAIN EXERCISE
Trainees will use copies of form included in the training manual and will fill the form out using the information they just recorded on the F.F. Style Scale.

5 MINUTES   HAVE TRAINEES READ FORM THOROUGHLY
Ask them if there are any questions.

20 MINUTES   HAVE TRAINEES FILL OUT SCORING FORM
Trainees should fill out the form following the instructions on the form.

15 MINUTES   DISCUSSION

TOTAL TIME: 25 MINUTES

Points to Look For

In the last section we discussed methods to assess the family's needs and aspirations. Just as important is identifying the family's strengths and special capabilities. This is the second of the four principles upon which family-level intervention is based.

As you may remember, these four principles are:
1. Specification and prioritization of family needs and aspirations
♦ **2. Utilization of existing family strengths and capabilities**
3. Identification of sources of support and resources for meeting needs and achieving aspirations
4. Effective help-giver roles in creating opportunities for the development of additional skills and competencies

Included in this section are:
- A discussion of the terms "Family Strengths" and "Family Functioning Style"
- Definitions of family strengths
- Qualities of strong families
- Methods for assessing family strengths
- Interviewing tips to help identify family functioning style

[?] Discussion Questions

As we focus on identification of family strengths and capabilities you should look for and remember the following important points.

❏ When using the term "strengths," a help-giver should be careful not to imply the opposite--weaknesses. For this reason, the term "Family Functioning Style" is used to refer to a family's unique combination of strengths and capabilities. *How can you focus on strengths, while avoiding comparisons to weaknesses?*

❏ A family is a system of individuals possessing capabilities. A help-giver should look for these resources in individual family members and strong points in the interactions among family members. *What are some signs of strengths and capabilities in a family?*

❏ Focusing on the family's good points rather than only on problems makes the intervention more positive. *How can you adapt your approach to intervention in order to focus more on strengths?*

❏ If a family can build on their good points, they are more likely to feel successful in meeting needs. *How can you encourage this success?*

Notes

STRENGTHS & CAPABILITIES

Families are unique in the ways they react to daily events of life and the ways that individual family members grow and interact. We, as help-givers who work with families, should realize that we can be of most benefit to families by promoting their unique abilities to identify and utilize their own family strengths.

When referring to family capabilities, however, we believe there is danger in using only the word "strengths" because that implies a continuum, with strengths at one end and weaknesses at the opposite end. We prefer the term "family functioning style" because it better describes the family's unique ways of dealing with life events and promoting growth and development. **The term "family functioning style" is used to refer to the combination of a family's strengths and its abilities to meet the needs of daily life.**

< Remember

With this warning in mind, let us now examine effective ways to identify family strengths and integrate them into interventions.

Family Strengths

A family's strengths, such as the ability to communicate well or the ability to solve problems, are resources for meeting daily needs. While this seems simple enough, it is surprising how little is known about family strengths. As Otto (1963) pointed out over 25 years ago:

> Although the professional literature is replete with criteria for identifying "problem families" and criteria useful in the diagnosis of family problems or family disorganization, little is known about how we might identify a "strong family." (p. 329)

In spite of the fact that few advances have been made since Otto first made this claim, it is our desire to give some guidelines which will begin to bridge this gap toward methods of identifying strong families and intrafamily strengths.

Think About It...

> Why is it important to identify family strengths?
>
> Why shouldn't help-givers just "solve problems?"

Implications

There are a number of implications to be drawn from what we do know about family strengths and family functioning style.

1. Recognizing the existence of the qualities of strong families calls attention to the fact that all families have strengths that are valuable resources.

2. Recognizing and employing family strengths as one way of meeting needs builds upon those strengths--the very things that make a family "work well" to begin with.

3. Building upon and strengthening the family's resources makes the family unit even stronger and more capable of directing the growth of individual family members and the family unit.

Definition of Family Strengths

According to Williams, Lindgren, Rowe, VanZandt, & Stinnet (1985):

"Family strengths refers to those relationship patterns, *interpersonal skills and competencies, and social and psychological characteristics* [italics added] which create a sense of positive family identity, promote satisfying and fulfilling interaction among family members, encourage the development of the potential of the family group and individual family members, and contribute to the family's ability to deal effectively with stress and crisis" (Preface).

Similarly, Otto (1975) defined family strengths as:

"...those *forces and dynamic factors* [italics added] ... which encourage the development of the personal resources and potentials of members of the family and which make family life deeply satisfying and fulfilling to family members" (p. 16).

These definitions suggest both that family strengths are interpersonal and intrafamilial in nature and that they are influenced by forces within and outside the family unit. This broad view of family strengths is consistent with the social systems approach which asserts that a family is a system of individuals within a larger framework of other human and societal systems.

Think About It...

> *Think of a family which you consider to be a strong, or healthy family. How do they compare to the following list?*

Qualities of Strong Families

The family strengths literature suggests that there are 12 major non-mutually exclusive qualities of strong families. Before listing these characteristics, however, it should be made explicitly clear that not all strong families are characterized by the presence of all the traits of a strong family **A strong family is likely to possess some combination of these qualities; this combination defines that family's unique family functioning style.**

According to *Assessing Family Strengths and Family Functioning Style (Trivette, Dunst, Deal, Hamer and Propst, 1989)*, the following are 12 traits of a strong family.

Pg 25 in Text.

1. A belief in and sense of <u>commitment</u> toward promoting the well-being and growth of individual family members as well as that of the family unit.

2. <u>Appreciation</u> for the small and large things that individual family members do well and encouragement to do better.

3. Concentrated effort to spend <u>time</u> and do things together, no matter how formal or informal the activity or event.

4. A sense of <u>purpose</u> that permeates the reasons and basis for "going on" in both bad and good times.

5. A sense of <u>congruence</u> among family members regarding the value and importance of assigning time and energy to what the family considers important goals, needs, projects, and functions.

6. The ability to <u>communicate</u> with one another in a way that emphasizes positive interaction among family members.

7. A clear set of family <u>rules, values, and beliefs</u> that establishes expectations about acceptable and desired behavior.

8. A varied repertoire of <u>coping strategies</u> that encourage positive functioning in dealing with both normative and non-normative life events.

9. The ability to engage in <u>problem-solving</u> activities designed to evaluate options for meeting needs and procuring resources.

10. The ability to be <u>positive</u> and see the positive in almost all aspects of their lives, including the ability to see crises and problems as opportunities to learn and grow.

11. <u>Flexibility</u> and <u>adaptability</u> in the roles necessary to procure resources to meet needs.

12. A <u>balance</u> between the use of internal and external family resources for coping and adapting to life events and planning for the future.

More information about the qualities of a strong family can be found in Curran's book, *Traits of a Healthy Family* (1983).

Stop and Practice Your Skills

Activity: Family Strengths Grid

Fill out the Family Strengths Grid below, drawing the information from your own family. You may want to give copies of this grid to other members of your family and ask them to fill it out also. This will provide you with an interesting comparison for discussion.

Write each strength on the grid below. In the boxes to the right of each strength you list, answer the corresponding questions. (e.g., Put a check for yes in line 1 under column "A" if the answer to question "A" is yes for strength #1, etc.) Leave the box blank if the answer is no.

Questions

A. Has any other family member ever mentioned this as a strength?
B. Do other family members know you consider this to be a strength?
C. Has this always been a strength of your family?
D. Has this strength been easy to develop?
E. Has this strength ever been tested?

Strengths	A	B	C	D	E

Source: Achord, B., Berry, M., Harding, G., Kerber, K., Scott, S., Schwab, L.O. (March, 1986). *All families have strengths.* Building Family Strengths Project at the Center for Family Strengths. Lincoln, Nebraska. (Adapted from: Simon, S.M. [1978] *Values Clarification.*)

Assessing Family Strengths

Family strengths can be assessed through interviews or through the use of a family strengths inventory and scale such as the one included in this manual. In almost every situation, an interview (or combination of interview and use of a scale) is preferable to use of a scale alone. In either case, the family members' responses should be used to prompt more discussion about the family's strengths.

While the qualities of the strong family listed previously are a helpful guideline, it is important to remember that most families--even strong families--will not display all these characteristics. As noted by Otto (1962), "Strengths are not isolated variables, but form clusters and constellations which are <u>dynamic, fluid, interrelated, and interacting</u>" (p. 80, emphasis added). When using family strengths scales, your discussion should focus on the way the family's qualities are interrelated and how they are used by the family to meet needs.

Remember

Family Strengths Inventory

The Family Strengths Inventory includes items that measure qualities of strong families and aspects of interpersonal and intrapersonal relationships. Each item is rated on a five-point scale according to the degree to which the quality or characteristic is present in the family. The scale yields a total scale score that provides a basis for determining overall family strengths.

It is the individual responses to the items, however, that are most useful for determining family functioning style. For example, a respondent might report that it is very characteristic for her family to deal with crises in a positive manner. The help-giver should then ask her for further details about how this occurs. For example, "You have said that your family deals with difficult situations in a positive way. Can you give me an example or tell me what helps your family see "good" even in times of difficulty?" The responses to more specific questions give the interviewer a better idea about how this quality contributes to family functioning style.

Family Strengths Scale

The Family Strengths Scale includes items that assess two dimensions of family functioning: <u>family pride</u> (loyalty, optimism, trust in the family) and <u>family accord</u> (ability to accomplish tasks, deal with problems, get along together). For each item, the respondent indicates the extent to which the quality is present in his or her family. The items tap strengths such as trust and confidence, ability to express feelings, congruence in values and beliefs, respect, etc.

Responses on individual items as well as subscale scores can be used as a way of asking families to describe the basis for why they consider particular characteristics to be family strengths. For example, "Could you tell me about how your family prevents problems from reoccurring in your household?" The response to this question will provide considerable insight into the family's unique functioning style.

The Family System

Identifying and mobilizing family strengths is most beneficial when:

- the family is viewed as a system of individual members or subunits with capabilities
- family strengths are seen as the combination and interaction of capabilities of individual family members
- family functioning style is defined as the unique clustering and integration of family strengths that help meet needs

A family system is made up of interconnected individuals (mother, father, children, etc.) who are sources of support to one another. The resources that each person possesses are the knowledge and skills that they have learned and acquired through interactions with others, both within and outside the family unit. The "richness" of a family's reservoir of resources is dependent on the range and variety of capabilities of individual family members.

> What is the difference between an interconnected family system and a group of people who just happen to live or work together?
>
> Is there a difference? If so, how does this affect family-level intervention?

When the family system is viewed as an integrated unit comprised of individual family members, family strengths become the sum of the strengths of individual family members either in combination or interaction. By combination we mean two or more family members working together, performing the <u>same or similar</u> tasks to achieve a desired goal (e.g., all family members "chipping in" and cleaning the house before visitors arrive). By interaction we mean two or more family members performing <u>different</u> tasks to make the family system work in the best interest of individual family members and the family unit as a whole (e.g., one person baby-sits so that another person is available to cook the meals without distraction).

The following conversation between a mother and a help-giver illustrates how the skills of individual family members can be used to help meet the family's needs.

Mother: I'm really worried about my father; we just put him in a nursing home and I'd like to visit him more often. I know he's lonely and I think he feels like we don't care. I just can't take the children with me and I can't always find a baby-sitter.

Help Giver: You were telling me last week about how your daughter was wanting to earn money for a school trip. Do you think she would be willing to stay with the younger children one evening a week so you could visit with your father?

Mother: I hadn't thought about that, but maybe Sandi could help. She is getting old enough to help make dinner and bathe the kids. And that would let her earn some money for her trip.

Help Giver: I'm sure Sandi has been a great support for you since you and your husband separated. Do you think she's mature enough to take on more responsibilities for household chores? This might allow you a little more flexibility.

Mother: It's been pretty hard to manage with the children and the the house all alone. But, I know Sandi is able to do more than I sometimes let her do. I'll talk with her this afternoon and see what we can work out.

What resources are identified in this conversation? Are these resources ones that are already available, but not fully used by the family? Will the resources help meet the family's needs?

What other resources might be available?

Tips From the Text

- A family is a system of individuals, each of whom possesses resources.

- Family strengths refer to factors which contribute to positive family identity and the development of necessary resources.

- A strong family exhibits some, but not necessarily all of the qualities of a strong family described in this section.

- Family strengths are important considerations in the intervention process, but should be considered part of the family's functioning style, or unique way of dealing with life events.

- Family functioning style refers to both the strengths possessed by a family and its individual members, and to the family's patterns of dealing with life events.

Methods for Identifying Family Functioning Style

Family functioning style may be identified either in an interview format or in an interview combined with any number of family strengths scales such as the one just reviewed. Either approach can be used to identify the things that individual family members and the family unit "do well." The help-giver should remember, however, that family functioning style includes both the presence of strengths or capabilities and the manner in which these skills are used by the family to secure or create resources.

Consider these three questions when assessing family functioning style:

1. Which of the qualities of strong families described in this section are displayed by the family?
2. How are strengths used as family resources for meeting needs?
3. How does the family use these as well as any other capabilities to mobilize or create extrafamily resources to meet needs?

As noted in Stoneman (1985), *"Every family has strengths and, if the emphasis is on supporting strengths rather than rectifying weaknesses, chances for making a difference in the lives of children and families are vastly increased"* (p. 462).

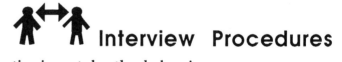 Interview Procedures

In an interview to determine family functioning style, the help-giver should pay particular attention to individual family member behavior and the interactions among family members. One may also pose questions in order to elicit descriptions of the things the family does which indicate family strengths, capabilities, and resources.

The following tips and strategies may help identify family strengths:

Observe behaviors of family members.

During an interview, family members may report few strengths directly, but at the same time, may display strengths through actions or examples. If the family members listen to one another and respectfully refrain from interruption, this indicates a sense of mutual respect. If a family member describes some project that the family is involved in (even if it is an illustration of some unrelated point), the interviewer should note that the family has a commitment to working together.

Observe the physical environment of the home.

Clues to family strengths and capabilities may be scattered all over the home, waiting to be discovered by the observant eye of the interviewer. Look for the "personal touch" of homemade crafts or decorations, special care given to entertaining and educating the children, extra effort put towards creating a healthy, happy home. These observations allow the interviewer to comment on the family's strengths and capabilities, and such comments can lead to further discussion about the family's functioning style.

Ask for a description of daily routines.

Daily chores and responsibilities, mealtime activities, leisure time in the evenings and on weekends ... . Information on daily activities and routines may reveal aspects of family functioning style which an interviewer may not think to ask about. You may want to find out who does what around the house, how time is spent together, how responsibilities of running a household are divided and shared. Pay close attention to the ways in which a family copes with both the enjoyable and the not-so-enjoyable tasks.

Ask questions which can lead to discussion of family strengths.

Questions such as "What do you enjoy doing together as a family?" and "Does your family share any hobbies or interests?" will open opportunities for a family to talk about activities which reflect their strengths. The family may not even realize that they are describing strengths as they describe interests and common activities.

Listen actively.

A family member may tell a funny story of some family incident, which could easily be laughed at and forgotten, but the active listener will pay attention to these anecdotes, looking for clues. Many family stories include descriptions of behaviors that may reflect the family's functioning style.

Restate negative points in a positive way.

Families who are in need of help often focus on their problems and have difficulty seeing the positive side of their family functioning style. The help-giver should look for alternative ways to view things and point out the positive aspects whenever possible. For example, if a family is having financial difficulty, look at the reasons why. Perhaps their money is going to support an elderly relative. Praise the family for positive efforts in a negative situation.

Point out family strengths and capabilities.

In addition to looking for the positive aspects of negative situations, you can directly point out to the family the strengths and capabilities you see in them. Perhaps they possess an ability to do something well, but have simply faced barriers in actually doing it. The family may believe that they are incapable, when actually outside circumstances have been the source of the problem. Reassurance from the help-giver can boost the family's confidence in their abilities.

Are there some standard questions you can have ready when you begin an interview?

What would you always want to ask?

Tips From the Text

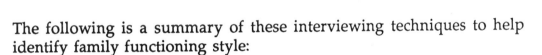

The following is a summary of these interviewing techniques to help identify family functioning style:

- Observe family behaviors to determine characteristics of family functioning style.

- Observe physical environment and comment on strengths displayed there.

- Ask about daily routines and activities.

- Ask specific questions which may get family members to describe events that reflect family strengths.

- Listen to family stories -- they may hold a wealth of information.

- Try to restate negative comments in a more positive manner. Emphasize positive aspects of each statement.

- Tell the family members what you see as their strengths, to encourage them and to help them see these strengths in themselves.

Stop and Practice Your Skills

Activity: Family Functioning Style Scale

The Family Functioning Style Scale is an instrument for measuring aspects of family strengths and for providing descriptive information about family strengths and capabilities. Before using the scale, the help-giver should discuss with the family the purpose of the scale and how the information will be used. By completing the scale, family members (and the help-giver working with the family) can gain a better understanding of the family's characteristics, but the scale should be used only as a prompt in clarifying family strengths and to emphasize the positive qualities of the family. The use of the scale with a family should always focus on qualities rather than numbers; scores indicate relative strengths, not weaknesses.

The purpose of this exercise is for trainees to experience completing the Family Functioning Style Scale. On the following pages you will find a set of blank forms to use for this practice exercise. Complete the Family Functioning Style Scale, following the instructions given on each page. Your trainer can give you further directions or answer specific questions, if needed.

Activity: Scoring Form

After you have completed the Family Functioning Style Scale, you may transfer the information to the Scoring form. This form (which follows the scale) is used to summarize the information on the Family Functioning Style Scale and includes spaces for individual item scores and subscale scores.

Follow the instructions on the form to transfer your information from the Family Functioning Style Scale. Again, your trainer can give you any further information you may need.

Pg 177 IN TEXT

FAMILY FUNCTIONING STYLE SCALE

Angela G. Deal   Carol M. Trivette   Carl J. Dunst

Family Name _____ Date _____

INSTRUCTIONS

Every family has unique strengths and capabilities, although different families have different ways of using their abilities. This questionnaire asks you to indicate whether or not your family is characterized by 26 different qualities. The questionnaire is divided into three parts. Part 1 below asks you about all the members of your immediate family (persons living in your household). Part 2 on the inside asks you to rate the extent to which different statements are true for your family. Part 3 on the last page asks you to write down the things that you think are your family's most important strengths.

Please list all the members of your immediate family and fill in the information requested. When you are finished, turn to the next page.

FAMILY MEMBER	DATE OF BIRTH	AGE	RELATIONSHIP

INSTRUCTIONS

Listed below are 26 statements about families. Please read each statement and indicate the extent to which it is true for your family (people living in your home). Please give your honest opinions and feelings. Remember that your family will not be like ALL the statements given.

How is your family like the following statements?	Not At All Like My Family	A Little Like My Family	Sometimes Like My Family	Usually Like My Family	Almost Always Like My Family
1. We make personal sacrifices if they help our family.......................	0	1	2	3	4
2. We agree about how family members should behave...........	0	1	2	3	4
3. We believe that something good comes out of even the worst situations.................................	0	1	2	3	4
4. We take pride in even the smallest accomplishments of family members...........................	0	1	2	3	4
5. We share our concerns and feelings in useful ways...................	0	1	2	3	4
6. Our family sticks together no matter how difficult things get......	0	1	2	3	4
7. We can ask for help from persons outside our family if needed....................................	0	1	2	3	4
8. We agree about the things that are important to our family...........	0	1	2	3	4
9. We are willing to "pitch in" and help each other...........................	0	1	2	3	4
10. We find things to do that keep our minds off our worries..............	0	1	2	3	4
11. We try to look "at the bright side of things"..	0	1	2	3	4
12. We find time to be together........	0	1	2	3	4
13. Everyone in our family understands the "rules" about acceptable ways to act..............	0	1	2	3	4

How is your family like the following statements?	Not At All Like My Family	A Little Like My Family	Sometimes Like My Family	Usually Like My Family	Almost Always Like My Family
14. Friends and relatives are willing to help whenever needed.........	0	1	2	3	4
15. Our family is able to make decisions about what to do when we have problems or concerns..............................	0	1	2	3	4
16. We enjoy time together...............	0	1	2	3	4
17. We try to forget our problems or concerns for a while when they seem overwhelming.....................	0	1	2	3	4
18. Family members are able to listen to both sides of the story.....	0	1	2	3	4
19. We make time to get things done that are important..............	0	1	2	3	4
20. We can depend on the support of each other whenever something goes wrong......	0	1	2	3	4
21. We talk about the different ways we deal with problems and concerns..................................	0	1	2	3	4
22. Our family's relationships will outlast material possessions........	0	1	2	3	4
23. We make decisions like moving or changing jobs for the good of all family members...................	0	1	2	3	4
24. We can depend on each other..	0	1	2	3	4
25. We try not to take each other for granted...............................	0	1	2	3	4
26. We try to solve our problems first before asking others to help.......	0	1	2	3	4

Please write down all things that you consider to be the major strengths of your family. Don't overlook the little things that occur every day which we often take for granted (e.g., sharing the responsibility of getting your child fed and to school).

FAMILY FUNCTIONING STYLE SCALE

SCORING FORM

Angela G. Deal   Carol M. Trivette   Carl J. Dunst

Respondent _____   Date _____   Recorder _____

DIRECTIONS
The scoring process is designed to facilitate accurate summarization of responses on The Family Functioning Style Scale. The scoring sheet includes spaces for individual item scores and subscale scores. The recorder should first enter the item scores (from the Family Functioning Style Scale) in the boxes on the scoring sheet and then sum each column to obtain the subscale scores. The subscale scores are written in the top "triangle" at the bottom of each column and compared to the total possible for each column.

SCORING FORM

ITEM	Commitment	Cohesion	Communication	Competence	Coping
1		☐			
2				☐	
3			☐		
4		☐			
5			☐		
6		☐			
7					☐
8			☐		
9	☐				
10					☐
11					☐
12	☐				
13					☐
14					☐
15					☐
16	☐				
17			☐		
18			☐		
19	☐				
20				☐	
21			☐		
22		☐			
23		☐			
24		☐			
25	☐				
26				☐	
Subscale Score / Total Possible	20	24	24	12	24

Support & Resources

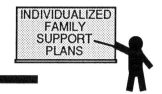

Trainer's Notes

Support & Resources continues to expand upon the four principles presented in **Working with Families**. Unlike the two prior principles which looked inside the family to identify family needs and strengths, this principle focuses outside the family to identify both informal and formal sources of social support. Following this section, **The Effective Help-Giver** will complete presentations on the model.

Time

For a training group of 10 people, allow 3 hours to discuss this section, answer questions, and complete any exercises or activities.

Materials

For this session you will need to have:

- training manual for *Developing Individualized Family Support Plans*

- *Enabling and Empowering Families* (Dunst, Trivette & Deal, 1988)

- chalkboard and chalk, flip-chart or newsprint and markers, along with masking tape to attach pieces of newsprint to the wall

- optional: overhead transparencies

- optional: overhead projector and screen or light-colored wall

Before You Begin

- Be sure all equipment is set up properly.

- Read the material covered in the Training Manual on **Support & Resources**.

- Complete all activities and thoroughly familiarize yourself with the Family Network Matrix by filling out all pages of the form based on a case study or by reviewing several completed matrices.

- Be prepared to discuss the questions below.

 ## Discussion Questions

❑ It is possible to differentiate between informal and formal sources of support, not only in terms of who is included in each of these groups, but also in terms of their availability to families in need. *Based on this information, why would you expect informal sources of support to families to be more effective?*

❑ According to the text, there are several ways in which social support (direct or indirect) influences child, parent, and family functioning. Can you think of other ways? *Drawing from your own experience, what are some positive influences of social support you have witnessed in working with families?*

❑ As a help-giver, your efforts in working with a family are directed toward the family's eventually assuming responsibility for meeting their own needs. *What are the implications for your work with families of the availability of different types of informal and formal support? How can you describe the relationships between social support and child, parent, and family functioning?*

Tips for Leading Discussion

- Ask if there are any questions from the reading.

- Ask trainees to share with the group some experiences they have had supporting a family in strengthening its informal support network. Did the family and the help-giver both find this a positive experience?

- Ask trainees to share ways they have altered or broadened their intervention practices (or plan to alter their intervention practices) in order to help families take better advantage of their informal support networks.

- It is important that trainees view and use forms like the Personal Network Matrix as adjuncts to one or more personal interviews, if they are used at all. Encourage trainees to discuss their use of/reliance on forms as assessment tools, always emphasizing their proper role.

- Encourage trainees to discuss the "costs" of asking for and accepting help, both from a personal point of view and from experience with clients.

- Be alert for trainees who seem uncomfortable with transferring support for families from formal agencies/professionals to informal networks. Be sure to point out that involving informal support sources does not mean there is not an important role for the professional.

Activities

There are three written activities in this section. The personal Network Matrix is reviewed but not completed as a group activity.

Preparation for all activities

Complete all activities ahead of time so you will be prepared to answer questions. Familiarize yourself with the Personal Network Matrix by filling one out or by reviewing several completed matrices.

Activity: Sources of Support

5 MINUTES	EXPLAIN ACTIVITY AND ANSWER QUESTIONS Trainees will add names/designations of individuals, groups, organizations, and agencies in each of the appropriate circles, using the examples given as a guide.
10 MINUTES	HAVE TRAINEES COMPLETE THE ACTIVITY
10 MINUTES	DISCUSSION What is the value of completing an exercise like this with clients? What can be said about the number, type, and availability of members of the informal network?

TOTAL TIME: 25 MINUTES

Activity: Who 'Ya Gonna Call?

5 MINUTES	EXPLAIN ACTIVITY AND ANSWER QUESTIONS Trainees will complete the exercise using themselves as clients. It is okay to have more than one response to each situation; just remind trainees to designate each response as formal or informal.
15 MINUTES	HAVE TRAINEES COMPLETE THE ACTIVITY
10 MINUTES	DISCUSSION Was it difficult to respond to any of the situations? Why? How large a role does lack of experience with certain situations play when resources are suddenly required in that area? (e.g., If you've never used an attorney or therapist, did you have someone in mind to call or did you know the best way to go about finding a good person?)

TOTAL TIME: 30 MINUTES

Activity: Mapping Your Family

5 MINUTES   EXPLAIN ACTIVITY

Each trainee will use the space provided to create a map of his or her own family within its social context. It is best to do this exercise around the trainee's present family (and not the family of origin) so that information about supports and stresses is current. Don't worry about having a neat map!!

5 MINUTES   ANSWER QUESTIONS

Use the maps in the text as guides. Encourage trainees to add "systems" such as work and transportation in addition to persons and organizations. Make connecting lines to individuals or to the family as a whole.

15 MINUTES   COMPLETE THE ACTIVITY

15 MINUTES   DISCUSSION

Focus on trainees and their connections to sources of support as well to systems which place demands on or cause stress for them. Emphasize the value of this activity with families in complex situations as a way of clarifying issues for them.

TOTAL TIME: 40 MINUTES

Points to Look For

The identification of sources of support and resources for meeting needs and achieving goals is the third principle of the family-level assessment and intervention process. Unlike the two prior principles which looked inside the family to identify needs and strengths, the focus of this principle lies primarily outside the family. Methods for identifying both informal and formal sources of support -- such as relatives, friends, community programs -- and resources of information and material aid to assist families in need are our concern in this section.

Again, the four principles are:

1. Specification and prioritization of family needs and aspirations
2. Utilization of existing family strengths and capabilities
❖ 3. **Identification of sources of support for meeting needs and achieving aspirations**
4. Effective help-giver roles in creating opportunities for the development of additional skills and competencies

The questions below anticipate the contents of this section of the training manual. You can use the back of this page to make your own notes or responses to the items below.

 **Discussion Questions**

❑ It is possible to differentiate between informal and formal sources of support, not only in terms of who is included in each of these groups, but also in terms of their availability to families in need. *Based on this information, why would you expect informal sources of support to families to be more effective?*

❑ According to the text, there are several ways in which social support (direct and indirect) influences child, parent, and family functioning. Can you think of other ways? *Drawing from your own experience, what are some positive influences of social support you have witnessed in working with families?*

❑ As a help-giver, your efforts in working with a family are directed toward the family's eventually assuming responsibility for meeting their own needs. *What are the implications for your work with families of the availability of different types of informal and formal support?   How can you describe the relationships between social support and child, parent, and family functioning?*

Notes

SUPPORT & RESOURCES

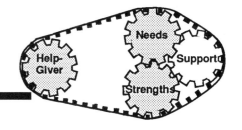

To a family, support can mean many things, from transportation to a doctor's appointment or admission for their child to a day care center to having access to another parent with a handicapped child who can understand the family's feelings or demonstrate ways of coping with the child's special needs and routines.

Sources of support can be identified along a continuum which begins with the family itself and progresses outward through networks of relatives, informal associations, professionals and organizations, to policy-making groups and individuals. While it is always best to look inside the family first for support and resources to meet needs, it is often necessary to look outside as well. How to help families find and obtain these resources will be the focus of this section.

Definitions

Extra-family resources and social support (resources and support from outside the nuclear family) include the emotional, physical, informational, instrumental, and material aid and assistance provided by others to families to help them meet their needs. Provision of needed support and resources promotes positive family functioning.

Keep in mind, also, the definitions below as you read the rest of this section. These conditions will virtually always influence the process of seeking and providing resources and support.

- **RESPONSE COSTS:** Extent to which the "benefits" of seeking and accepting help are outweighed by the "costs" (the risks of asking for help, the sense of indebtedness that may be felt) to the family

- **DEPENDABILITY:** Extent to which network members are willing to provide aid so the family can depend on them in times of need

- **INDEBTEDNESS:** Extent to which a personal or psychological sense of obligation is created by support provided by a network member

- **RECIPROCITY:** Extent to which mutually beneficial support may be exchanged between family and network members, but is not expected

- **SATISFACTION:** Extent to which the family finds help provided by network members meets the needs they identified and prioritized

Information about conceptual frameworks for specifying components of support may be found in the accompanying text, pp 28-30.

Stop and Practice Your Skills

Activity: Sources of Support

The diagram below represents the family embedded within other systems, members of which are or may be sources of support to the family. At each of the four levels beyond the immediate family there are individuals or groups who belong to the designated network. (For example, in-laws belong to the kinship network and church members belong to the informal network.)

Write in as many potential members for each network as occur to you, in addition to those already written in below.

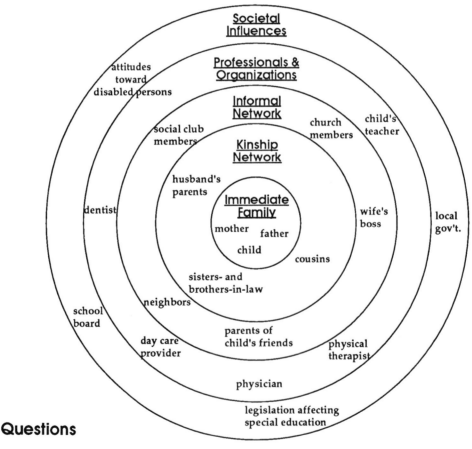

Questions

- Was it helpful to visualize family support networks in this way?

- When might you use this exercise for some families you work with?

- If the informal network level is the fullest, does that help to explain why informal sources of support are so valuable to families?

Informal and Formal Sources of Support

Many sources of support and resources available to a family appear in the network circles on the facing page. They include relatives, friends, neighbors, co-workers, church members, clubs and social organizations, day care centers, and any other individual, group, or organization that the family has contact with either directly or indirectly.

Informal Support

Operationally, we can differentiate between informal and formal sources of support by considering how contact is made, availability of the support, and often by the level of technicality or expertise which is being sought. Informal support sources include individuals (friends, relatives, neighbors, co-workers, etc.) and groups (churches, social clubs, parent organizations, etc.). Informal sources of support are available without contact through a professional or agency to provide support for needs associated with daily living, in response to both routine and emergency life events.

Formal Support

Formal support networks include both professionals (physicians, infant specialists, social workers, therapists, etc.) and agencies (hospitals, early intervention programs, health departments, day care centers, etc.). These sources of support and resources are usually available to families through formal channels during regular working hours. While there are certain services which should be provided by members of the formal support network -- medical treatment for any complicated or serious condition or psychotherapy, for example -- formal support systems should not be the primary sources of support to the family.

Effects of Informal Support

Research regarding the effects of support provided by both formal and informal sources, regardless of the population being studied, has demonstrated at least one consistent finding: the positive effects of support provided by informal sources (i.e., that provided by personal network members) generally exceed the positive effects of support attributed to formal support sources. In other words, informal support provided to families effectively helps to promote family and individual health and well-being while relieving stress and need which interfere with positive family functioning.

When you need help for yourself or for someone in your family, how do you consider where or to whom you will turn for this help?

Stop and Practice Your Skills

Activity: Who 'Ya Gonna Call?

Imagine yourself in each of the circumstances described below. Who would you turn to for help? Write the name(s) of the person/agency in the space to the left of each description.

_____ • Your telephone doesn't work and you need to make an emergency phone call.

_____ • You find out you just won a free trip to Hawaii.

_____ • You discover a red, bumpy rash on your daughter's body.

_____ • You and your parents have just had a fight.

_____ • You have a flat tire on the interstate driving home from work.

_____ • Your neighbors inform you they are suing you for invading their privacy because you make too much noise in your home.

_____ • You need to find a new job.

_____ • You feel depressed.

_____ • You want to go back to school.

Now go back through your responses; circle those who belong to your informal support network and "check" formal sources of support.

Questions

1. Did you list more formal or more informal support sources?

2. Why did you choose formal support in some instances but informal support in others?

3. Were there situations where you were unsure of whom to turn to for help?

4. When you were unsure of whom to turn to for help, how would you have felt if you had been told whom to contact without any discussion or consideration of how you felt about the situation?

5. Do you think you responded differently from your colleagues to this activity because of your own life experiences and your personal network?

Identifying Support & Resources

Father: I'm dreading the start of the new school year. The children need some new clothes and I just don't have any money to spare right now to get them any. If my wife were still living she could make them something fine for almost nothing with her sewing machine.

Help-Giver: Is that how the two of you took care of the children's clothing needs in the past? Did your wife always make all their clothes?

Father: She made a lot of their clothes. But she'd also look out for nice second-hand clothes at garage or yard sales.

Help-Giver: Do you know of any family members or friends with children you could talk to about some clothes?

Father: There's one nice family at church with children a little older than my two -- sometimes they all play together. But I don't know about asking for clothes, not when I can't pay for them. I don't think I could do that.

Help-Giver: Can you think of anything you could offer in exchange for some school clothes for your children?

Father: Well, maybe if they needed any carpentry work done around the house, I could do some on the weekend. I don't know though ... .

One week later

Father: You know what? That nice family at church had a whole day's worth of work for me to do on their new house, and in exchange my children have good clothes -- good as new -- to start school in this fall.

Interview Goals

The most effective way to help a family identify sources of support and resources is during a face-to-face interview. The interviewer must know what questions to ask, be a skilled listener, and have the knowledge and resources to make suggestions for linking families with needed support. The dialogue above helps illustrate this process.

Interview procedures are an important part of working with families which will be addressed in greater detail in the next section of this manual, **The Effective Help-Giver**. At this time it will be useful, though, to consider some specific guidelines for assisting families in identifying sources of support and resources for meeting needs.

IDENTIFY THE FAMILY'S PERSONAL NETWORK. Help the family generate a list of people, groups, agencies, and organizations with whom they have regular contact or to whom they turn in times of need. This is the family's personal social network and has both formal and informal members. (See the "Personal Network Matrix" and "Mapping.")

DETERMINE PREVIOUS SOURCES OF SUPPORT. Ask the family, "Who has helped you before with a similar problem?" or, "Have you already talked to a friend or relative about what's bothering you?" or, "Have you thought about contacting someone at XYZ agency about ... ?" You may gain insight into how the family goes about identifying support.

MATCH PRIORITIZED NEEDS WITH POTENTIAL SOURCES OF SUPPORT. Look first within the family itself for resources to meet needs, then to other members of the family's informal and formal support network. Proceed down the family's prioritized list of needs as potential support is identified. The family should eventually assume this task.

EXPLORE SOURCES OF SUPPORT OUTSIDE THE FAMILY NETWORK. When needed aid is not available from existing network members, suggest resources you are familiar with to broaden the family's potential pool of support. For example, you may know a parent who has learned to cope well with her child's handicap and who might be a good source of information to the family about managing their handicapped child.

HELP REMOVE OBSTACLES THAT BLOCK NECESSARY SUPPORT. On some occasions identified sources of support don't appear to the family to be viable options for meeting needs because they seem too difficult to obtain. Help the family identify ways to overcome these secondary obstacles in order to obtain resources to meet their original needs.

For example, a parent who finds day care for her child may not be able to use this needed service if she has no way to get her child to the day care center. You might help the parent find someone already driving another child who could give her child a ride also.

DETERMINE THE "COST" OF SEEKING/ACCEPTING HELP. Asking for and accepting help are complicated processes for most people. A family may have a need for which necessary resources are available, yet the "cost" of asking for help, the perceived reliability or unreliability of the source of support, and the indebtedness which the family expects to feel may all interfere with the need being met.

 Always find out how the family feels about asking for/accepting help and what they perceive will be the response of those asked to give help. This information can allow you to explore with the family ways to manage obstacles that interfere with acquiring necessary resources.

MOVE THE FAMILY TO ACT ON OBTAINING IDENTIFIED RESOURCES. Once existing (or even potential) sources of support have been identified, assist the family in devising a plan for action to obtain the resources. Take as much advantage as possible of the family's existing strengths and capabilities in the methods selected for carrying out these actions. In most cases, plans for obtaining aid or assistance should be contingent upon the family playing an active role on their own behalf.

When participating in the efforts above, keep these important tips in mind:

- Focus efforts to obtain support and resources first within the family and next on the family's informal support network -- always at the closest possible level to the family unit itself.

- Do not use or create a professional resource for support if the same assistance can be provided by a member of the family's informal social network.

- Use professional services for support or resources which cannot be provided otherwise.

- Encourage the family to take as much responsibility as possible in identifying and obtaining needed resources.

- Create opportunities for the family to develop additional skills and capabilities as they identify and acquire needed support and resources.

Tools for Identifying Support and Resources

While face-to-face contact and the use of good interviewing skills are always the most effective and the preferred ways for working with families to identify sources of support and resources, the use of a written instrument can often supplement this process. **It is important to remember that scales, matrices, and other forms cannot adequately substitute for the skilled interview and so should be used sparingly and only to augment the information obtained during the interview.**

The Personal Network Matrix

The Personal Network Matrix is a tool for identifying personal network members who are providing or could provide support for meeting needs. It provides insight into frequency of contact with potential sources of support, availability of support sources for help with varied needs, and dependability of these resources for providing support.

The following page contains an explanation of and directions for completing each part of the matrix. This is followed by a copy of the matrix itself so you can follow along with the explanation.

PART 1 OF THE PERSONAL NETWORK MATRIX. This part of the matrix, page 1, asks the respondent to indicate how often he/she has had contact with each member of a list of potential sources of support within the last month. Contact may have been one-on-one, in a group, or over the telephone. There is room at the bottom of the page for the respondent to list other support sources not already on this list.

Completing this part of the matrix gives a measure of <u>frequency of contact</u> between the person in need and potential sources of support.

PART 2 OF THE PERSONAL NETWORK MATRIX. The second part of the matrix, pages 2-3, gives a more in-depth look at which support network members may actually provide aid or assistance to meet specific needs.

In order to complete part 2, the respondent lists up to 10 projects. ("Projects" is a term for needs or goals identified by the respondent as priorities for devotion of his/her own time and energy and for which support or resources are required. Projects may include finding a job, taking a vacation, teaching one's child to eat independently, making a budget, etc.) After listing the 10 projects, the respondent indicates with a check mark in the appropriate boxes which particular person(s) or group(s) he/she could go to or is going to for help with each project.

When completed, part 2 presents a graphic display of potential and actual sources of support for meeting specific needs -- a representation of support by type and by source.

PART 3 OF THE PERSONAL NETWORK MATRIX. The final part of the matrix measures the respondent's evaluation of how dependable the listed sources of support are in terms of providing help or assistance when needed.

When completed by a family member with the assistance of the help-giver, the Personal Network Matrix can assist both in identifying sources of support for meeting needs and achieving goals.

TIPS:
- Encourage the respondent to personalize the matrix and make it more specific by substituting names of designated individuals and agencies.
- If the choices for potential support are not appropriate/adequate, add names in blank spaces at the bottom of the page, or cross out unused listings and add the respondent's own support members.
- Help the respondent identify potential sources of support who are not being tapped for assistance, especially if some support members seem "overloaded."

PERSONAL NETWORK MATRIX

(Version 2)

Carol M. Trivette & Carl J. Dunst

Name_____ Date_____

This questionnaire asks about people and groups that may provide you help and assistance. The scale is divided into three parts. Please read the instructions that go with each part before completing each section of the questionnaire.

Listed below are different individuals and groups that people often have contact with face-to-face, in a group, or by telephone. Please indicate for each source listed how often you have been in contact with each person or group during the *past month*. Please indicate any person or group with whom you have had contact not included on our list.

How frequently have you had contact with each of the following during the *past month*	Not At All	Once Or Twice	Up To 10 Times	Up To 20 Times	Almost Every Day
1. Spouse or Partner	1	2	3	4	5
2. My Children	1	2	3	4	5
3. My Parents	1	2	3	4	5
4. Spouse or Partner's Parents	1	2	3	4	5
5. My Sister/Brother	1	2	3	4	5
6. Spouse or Partner's Sister/Brother	1	2	3	4	5
7. Other Relatives	1	2	3	4	5
8. Friends	1	2	3	4	5
9. Neighbors	1	2	3	4	5
10. Church Members	1	2	3	4	5
11. Minister, Priest, or Rabbi	1	2	3	4	5
12. Co-Workers	1	2	3	4	5
13. Baby Sitter	1	2	3	4	5
14. Day Care or School	1	2	3	4	5
15. Private Therapist for Child	1	2	3	4	5
16. Child/Family Doctors	1	2	3	4	5
17. Early Childhood Intervention Program	1	2	3	4	5
18. Hospital/Special Clinics	1	2	3	4	5
19. Health Department	1	2	3	4	5
20. Social Service Department	1	2	3	4	5
21. Other Agencies	1	2	3	4	5
22. _____	1	2	3	4	5
23. _____	1	2	3	4	5

Source: C.J. Dunst, C.M. Trivette, and A.G. Deal (1988). *Enabling and Empowering Families: Principles and Guidelines for Practice.* Cambridge, MA: Brookline Books. May be reproduced.

INSTRUCTIONS
This part of the scale asks you to do two things: (1) Begin by listing up to 10 needs or activities that are of concern to you. We call these things projects because they require our time and energy. Projects include things like finding a job, paying the bills, finishing school, playing with our children, going on vacation, teaching our child how to eat, and so on. (2) After you have listed up to 10

Which person or groups to the right would you go to for help with any of these projects: **PROJECTS**	Myself	Spouse or Partner	My Children	My Parents	Spouse or Partner's Parents	Sister/ Brother	Spouse or Partner's Sister/ Brother	Other Relatives
1.								
2.								
3.								
4.								
5.								
6.								
7.								
8.								
9.								
10.								

INSTRUCTIONS

projects, please indicate which persons or groups you could go to if you need help with any of the projects. Indicate who would provide you help by checking the appropriate box for the person or group that you would ask.

Friends	Neighbors	Church Members/ Minister	Co-Workers	Babysitter, Day Care, or School	Private Therapist for Child	Child/ Family Doctors	Early Childhood Intervention Program	Health Depart.	Social Services Depart.	Other Agencies

Whenever a person needs help or assistance, he or she generally can depend upon certain persons or groups more than others. Listed below are different individuals, groups, and agencies that you might ask for help or assistance. For each source listed, please indicate to what extent you could depend upon each person or group if you needed any type of help.

To what extent can you depend upon any of the following for help or assistance when you need it:	Not At All	Some times	Occasionally	Most of the Time	All of the Time
1. Spouse or Partner	1	2	3	4	5
2. My Children	1	2	3	4	5
3. My Parents	1	2	3	4	5
4. Spouse or Partner's Parents	1	2	3	4	5
5. My Sister/Brother	1	2	3	4	5
6. Spouse or Partner's Sister/Brother	1	2	3	4	5
7. Other Relatives	1	2	3	4	5
8. Friends	1	2	3	4	5
9. Neighbors	1	2	3	4	5
10. Church Members	1	2	3	4	5
11. Minister, Priest, or Rabbi	1	2	3	4	5
12. Co-Workers	1	2	3	4	5
13. Baby Sitter	1	2	3	4	5
14. Day Care or School	1	2	3	4	5
15. Private Therapist for Child	1	2	3	4	5
16. Child/Family Doctors	1	2	3	4	5
17. Early Childhood Intervention Program	1	2	3	4	5
18. Hospital/Special Clinics	1	2	3	4	5
19. Health Department	1	2	3	4	5
20. Social Service Department	1	2	3	4	5
21. Other Agencies	1	2	3	4	5
22. _____	1	2	3	4	5
23. _____	1	2	3	4	5

Source: C.J. Dunst, C.M. Trivette, and A.G. Deal (1988). *Enabling and Empowering Families: Principles and Guidelines for Practice.* Cambridge, MA: Brookline Books. May be reproduced.

Mapping

Mapping is another method which can be used by the help-giver and the family to assist in identifying sources of support and sources of tension or drain on family resources. Mapping is the process of creating a graphic representation of the family as it exists amid the individuals, groups, organizations, and agencies which it influences and which are influenced by it. In other words, mapping creates a picture of the family as a system that interacts with and is acted upon by other systems.

For more information about family mapping, see Hartman, A., & Laird, J. (1983). *Family-centered social work practice*. New York: Free Press.

Mapping can also be used to indicate the strength or weakness of the family's attachments to other network systems, as well as attachments which are particularly stressful or particularly supportive. The process of creating a family map is one which is best carried out with the family, and in fact can contribute considerable insight into the family situation for family members. An example of a family map appears below.

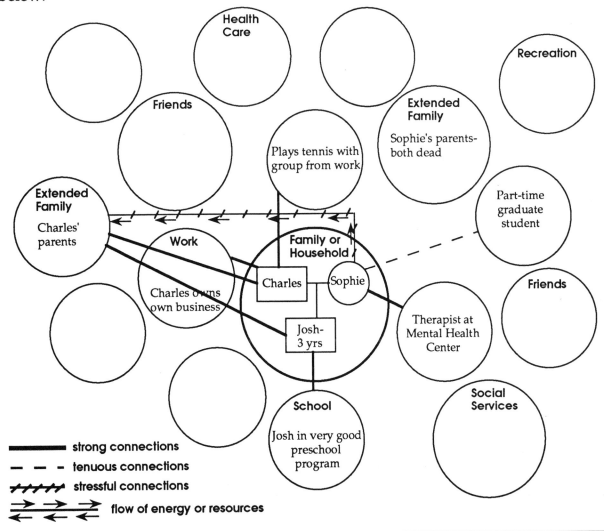

[handwritten margin note: Family as a system that interacts and is acted upon by other systems.]

In the example on the previous page, the nuclear family or household is represented by the large center circle (females in circles and males in squares), while surrounding systems are labelled and their relationship shown to the family by the type of connecting line (thick lines = strong connections; broken lines = tenuous connections; and hatched lines = stressful connections).

Arrows or key words written along the connecting lines indicate energy or support flowing to or away from the family or family member.

We can read the map above and determine these things:

- Charles and Sophie are married and have a son, Josh, 3 years old.
- Sophie's parents are both dead. Charles' parents are both living and have a strong relationship with both Charles and Josh, but a strained relationship with Sophie, though much energy is going from Sophie to Charles' parents.
- Charles has social outlets and rewarding work.
- Josh, who is mildly retarded, is in a good preschool program.
- Sophie does not work outside the home, but does have a tenuous connection to school.
- Sophie is also connected to a mental health worker.

On the facing page is another family map. Try to "read" the map before continuing this page and compare your interpretations to those below.

- Will, 45, is married to Ora, 39, and they have six children, all but one living at home.
- The youngest child, Dawn, is developmentally disabled but does not receive treatment regularly, perhaps because of transportation difficulties.
- Will is a night watchman and does odd jobs to supplement his income. He has social outlets through hunting with friends.
- Although the family owns its small home, they depend on food stamps and receive inconsistent health care from free clinics.
- No extended family are available to provide support, since Will's parents are dead and his siblings adopted and Ora's parents live out of state.
- One school-age child has learning disabilities and another attends a school where the vocational training he seeks is not offered.

Remember that these maps do not reveal a complete family picture (intra-family strengths are not represented, for example). Yet coupled with a personal interview, they can be very enlightening for the family and the help-giver.

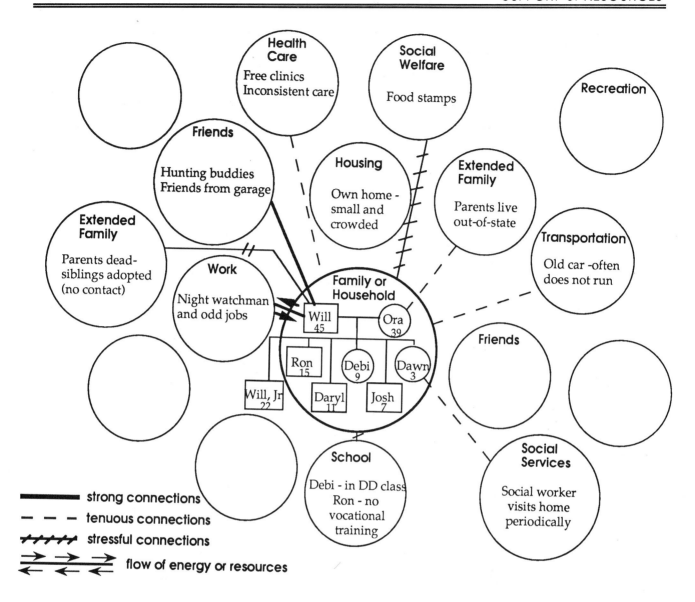

Health Care
Free clinics
Inconsistent care

Social Welfare
Food stamps

Recreation

Friends
Hunting buddies
Friends from garage

Housing
Own home -
small and
crowded

Extended Family
Parents live
out-of-state

Extended Family
Parents dead-
siblings adopted
(no contact)

Transportation
Old car -often
does not run

Work
Night watchman
and odd jobs

Family or Household
Will 45
Ora 39
Ron 15
Debi 9
Dawn 3
Will, Jr 22
Daryl 11
Josh 7

Friends

School
Debi - in DD class
Ron - no
vocational
training

Social Services
Social worker
visits home
periodically

Legend:
——— strong connections
– – – tenuous connections
+++++ stressful connections
⇒ flow of energy or resources

Think About It...

How would you involve a family directly in making a family map?

Can you see how this map could be very useful in complex family situations to illustrate for family members the presence or absence of needed sources of support?

Stop and Practice Your Skills

Activity: Mapping Your Family

Using the previous maps as guides, fill in this blank map of your own family, adding systems and connecting lines wherever needed. Pay careful attention to your own place on the map and your connections.

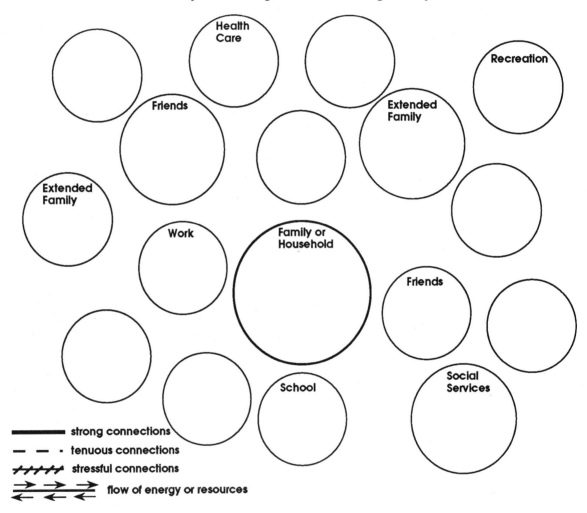

Questions

- Were you surprised by any information represented on the map?

- Does your position on the map show that you are taking care of yourself? Not more energy going out than what is coming in? Good support systems?

- Can you see how it could be helpful for families to visualize their family map, especially in complex situations where it might be difficult to think about all the connections?

Support, Resources, and Family Functioning

It should be helpful now to step back from the specific issues of identifying and obtaining support and look at the bigger picture of how support exerts an overall effect on families in need. The figure below represents the ways in which support from the family's personal network most often influences family functioning. According to this model:

1. Social support influences personal well-being and health (particularly that of the parents who are most often in direct contact with support systems).

2. Social support and enhanced parental well-being have positive effects on family functioning.

3. Social support, enhanced parental well-being, and improved family functioning influence the quality and types of parent-child interactions.

4. Social support, enhanced parental well-being, improved family functioning, and positive parent-child interactions have significant influences on child behavior and development.

Social support is usually most direct in terms of its influence on the health and well-being of the parents and most indirect in its influence on child behavior and development, though the effects of support are experienced throughout the family system.

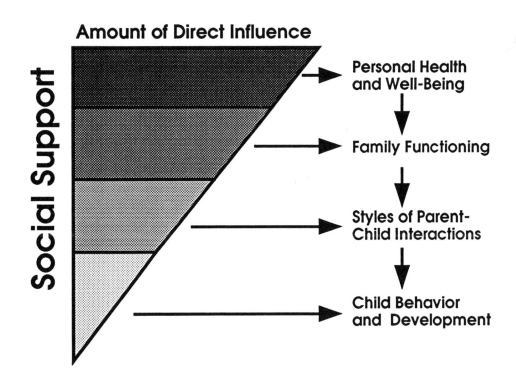

Adequate support, provided to families in need when they are lacking necessary resources, is vital to both short-term and long-term goals for handicapped children and their families. Improving the health and well-being of the family -- especially the parents -- can in turn lead to:

- decreased negative effects from time and energy demands placed upon a family by a disabled or at-risk child, which can

- promote positive exchanges and interactions among and between parents and children, which can

- enhance the parents' positive perception of their child's functioning and capabilities, which can

- influence a number of child behavior characteristics, such as affect, temperament, and motivation.

Implications for Effective Intervention Practices

The recognition and availability of various types of informal and formal family support and an understanding of the relationships between social support and parent, family, and child functioning have implications for how the effective help-giver intervenes with families in need. Three important conclusions we can draw are:

First, the operational definition of intervention itself must be expanded to include the many types of help and assistance provided by members of both the family's formal and informal support network.

Second, help-givers cannot afford to overlook or fail to take advantage of the pool of potential support available to a family in need from members of the family's personal support network.

Third, help-givers must strive to match resources to needs with particular attention to the increased use of informal sources of support. Supporting and strengthening the family's personal support network is one of the best ways of encouraging the family's ability to meet its own needs in the future.

Tips From the Text

Formal and Informal Sources of Support

Informal sources of support to families are an integral part of their daily lives, available to provide support for both routine and non-routine life events. These include (but are not limited to):

- relatives
- friends
- neighbors
- co-workers
- church members and clergy
- clubs and social organizations

Formal support networks include professionals and agencies who are organized to provide aid and assistance to families identified as being in need. Formal sources of support include:

- physicians
- infant specialists
- social workers
- therapists
- hospitals
- early intervention programs
- health departments

The positive effects of support provided by informal support sources generally outweigh the effects of support provided by formal networks.

Identifying Support and Resources

The most effective way to help families identify potential sources of assistance and support is through the personal interview. The goals of this interview are to:

- Identify the family's personal network.
- Determine previous sources of support.
- Match prioritized needs with potential sources of support.
- Explore sources of support outside the family network.

- Remove obstacles that block necessary support.
- Determine the "cost" of seeking and accepting help.
- Move the family to act on identified resources.

Instruments like the Personal Network Matrix and skills like the ability to "map" a family within its social context can be effectively coupled with the personal interview to assist families in identifying possible sources of aid and support.

Support, Resources, & Family Functioning

The provision of adequate support by the family's personal network directly and indirectly influences child, parent, and family functioning in a number of ways, such as:

- by enhancing personal health and well-being, especially of the parents who are most often in direct contact with support systems
- by positively affecting family functioning
- by improving the quality and types of parent-child interactions
- by influencing child behavior and development

The availability of a variety of formal and informal support sources and the interplay between social support and family functioning have implications for family intervention practices.

- First, the operational definition of intervention itself must be expanded to include the many types of help and assistance provided by members of both the family's formal and informal support network.

- Second, help-givers cannot afford to overlook or fail to take advantage of the pool of potential support available to a family in need from members of the family's personal support network.

- Third, help-givers must strive to match resources to needs with particular attention to the increased use of informal sources of support. Supporting and strengthening the family's personal support network is one of the best ways of encouraging the family's ability to meet its own needs in the future.

The Effective Help-Giver

Trainer's Notes

The previous three sections of the manual have examined the process of assessing the family's needs, strengths, and resources. In this section, the focus shifts from the help-seekers (the family) to the help-giver. This section contains several lists -- some rather lengthy -- so it is important to not let them overwhelm you or the trainees. Focus on applying the items on the lists (characteristics, roles, guidelines) to real-life experiences.

Time

For a training group of 10 people, allow 2 hours to discuss this section, answer questions, and complete any exercises or activities.

Materials

For this session you will need:

- training manual for *Developing Individualized Family Support Plans*

- *Enabling and Empowering Families* (Dunst, Trivette & Deal, 1988)

- chalkboard and chalk, flip-chart or newsprint and markers, along with masking tape to attach pieces of newsprint to the wall

- optional: overhead transparencies

- optional: overhead projector and screen or light-colored wall

Before You Begin

- Be sure all equipment is set up properly.

- Read the material covered in the Training Manual on **The Effective Help-Giver**.

- Complete the activities so you can answer questions about them.

- Be prepared to discuss the questions below.

 Discussion Questions

❑ Seven basic characteristics of effective help-seeker and help-giver exchanges are described in this section. *How are these characteristics interrelated? How would the absence of any one characteristic affect the help-giver/help-seeker relationship?*

❑ There are a number of roles which the help-giver can and does undertake when working with families in need. These roles can overlap and are often intermingled, yet they require specific skills of the help-giver. *Which of these roles are you most comfortable with? Which do you need to practice?*

❑ Offering help and accepting help are often complex processes that have psychological and social consequences for both parties involved. The guidelines presented here for enabling and empowering families aim to make that process as positive as possible. *How will you use these guidelines in your daily work?*

Tips for Leading Discussion

• Ask if there are any questions from the reading.

• Ask trainees to share with the group some experiences they have had as help-givers. Relate stories shared by trainees to the various characteristics of effective exchanges or to one or more of the help-giver roles. <u>Remember to positively reinforce the trainees' efforts toward becoming effective help-givers.</u>

• Emphasize the importance of enabling and empowering the family to solve its own problems and to meet its own needs. Use the guidelines for help-giving interventions along with examples from your own experience or from the trainees' experiences to reinforce these principles.

Activities

There are two activities in this section.

Preparation for all activities

Complete both activities ahead of time from your own experience so you will be prepared to answer questions.

Activity: Help-Giver/Help-Seeker Matrix

5 MINUTES   EXPLAIN ACTIVITY AND ANSWER QUESTIONS
Trainees will use the space provided to complete the matrix from their own personal experiences.

12 MINUTES   HAVE TRAINEES COMPLETE THE ACTIVITY

13 MINUTES   DISCUSSION
Focus on feelings described by trainees in each scenario. Are they comfortable discussing their own and other's feelings?

TOTAL TIME: 30 MINUTES

Activity: Enabling and Empowering Families

5 MINUTES   EXPLAIN ACTIVITY
Trainees will use the Guidelines for Help-Giving Interventions and real-life experiences to evaluate the effectiveness of the guidelines. Give two examples each of instances when specific guidelines were followed and the consequences and when guidelines were not followed and the consequences.

5 MINUTES   REVIEW FORM AND ANSWER QUESTIONS
Experiences may be the trainee's own or other actual cases with which they are familiar. The purpose of the exercise is to relate observing the guidelines with specific outcomes for the family or for the help-giving relationship.

15 MINUTES   COMPLETE THE ACTIVITY

15 MINUTES   DISCUSSION
Encourage trainees to share positive experiences from following the guidelines. How difficult will it be to adopt these methods for interventions? If there are examples that don't support the guidelines, does that mean they are not effective?

TOTAL TIME: 40 MINUTES

Points to Look For

The previous three sections of this manual have focused on identifying the needs and goals of the family, assessing the family's existing capabilities for meeting those needs, and determining what extra-family resources are available to provide support. The fourth component of the model presented here for working with families centers on the role of the help-giver during the intervention process.

Again, these four components are:

1. Specification and prioritization of family needs and aspirations
2. Utilization of existing family strengths and capabilities
3. Identification of sources of support for meeting needs and achieving aspirations
✧ **4. Effective help-giver roles in creating opportunities for the development of additional skills and competencies**

In the illustration above which uses the analogy of four interlocking gears, the effective help-giver is shown separate from, although connected to, the other three "gears." This component of the training centers on you the help-giver, rather than the family seeking help.

Keep in mind the questions below as you work through this section on **The Effective Help-Giver**. As always, you can use the back of this page to make your own notes or responses to the items below.

Discussion Questions

❑ Seven basic characteristics of effective help-seeker and help-giver exchanges are described in this section. *How are these characteristics interrelated? How would the absence of any one characteristic affect the help-giver/help-seeker relationship?*

❑ There are a number of roles which the help-giver can and does undertake when working with families in need. These roles can overlap and are often intermingled, yet they require specific skills of the help-giver. *Which of these roles are you most comfortable with? Which do you need to practice?*

❑ Offering help and accepting help are often complex processes that have psychological and social consequences for both parties involved. The guidelines presented here for enabling and empowering families aim to make that process as positive as possible. *How will you use these guidelines in your daily work?*

Notes

THE EFFECTIVE HELP-GIVER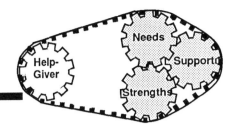

The approach we are presenting in this training module for working with families is sometimes characterized as proactive -- "pro" or positive in a number of ways, such as:

- viewing all families in a positive light

- promoting skills for self-reliance and independence

- encouraging the growth of all family members, not just the child whose needs brought the family to the attention of the help-giver

- acceptance of individual differences

- building on family strengths and capabilities in a way that supports and strengthens family functioning

- promoting the acquisition of knowledge and skills that make the family more competent

Another difference between this approach and other more traditional approaches to working with families has to do with intervention goals. The goals presented here for intervention are focused on positive outcomes -- developing and strengthening family functioning -- rather than on negative outcomes (e.g., prevention strategies which aim to decrease the risk of problems occurring and treatment strategies which attempt to correct problems).

Working within this framework to meet the individualized needs of families calls on the help-giver to function in both new and expanded roles. To enable, empower, support, and strengthen families in a way that makes <u>them</u> more able to find the resources to meet their needs requires a significant change in the role the professional help-giver typically assumes in family interactions.

Fortunately, this new role is one that can be learned and perfected with time and practice. While this is not always an easy process, it can be mastered, and the benefits of helping families become independent and self-sustaining make it rewarding.

Effective Help-Seeker/Help-Giver Exchanges

Exchanges between a family (help-seekers) and the help-giver must bear certain attributes if they are to assist the family in their efforts to become self-sustaining and if they are to contribute to the development of the new skills and approaches outlined here for the help-giver. Although we referred briefly to these characteristics in **Needs & Aspirations**, it is worthwhile considering them here in more detail.

Relationship

If there is not a mutual, trusting, open relationship between the help-giver and the family it will be virtually impossible for the help-giver to truly listen to the real needs of the family or for the family to feel confident enough to take the necessary risks to achieve goals and meet needs that up to this time have seemed insurmountable.

A healthy help-seeker/help-giver relationship is a partnership with all members working to achieve common goals. Every contact with the family contributes to or detracts from this partnership. And it is this partnership which creates the arena in which effective work with families can be achieved.

Communication

The most effective tool for building the type of help-seeker/help-giver relationship we have just described is through the use of good communication skills. Good communication employs the use of active and reflective listening techniques and open-ended questioning. **Good communication is based on trust and respect and is manifested not only in words but in actions and attitudes.**

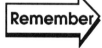

Honesty

Partnerships not based on trust and honesty are doomed to failure. Communication which is not founded on openness and honesty will either cease to exist or will turn to the detriment of both parties involved. For instance, whenever you meet with the family, state clearly the purpose of the encounter, what you are trying to achieve, and how any information they provide will be used.

Every communication with the family should be up-front and honest; when your caring and interest have been demonstrated, families will be open and honest in return. Failure to communicate honestly demonstrates disrespect for the family and is not facilitative in building a relationship.

Is it more difficult to be completely honest with a family when bad news must be shared?

Why is it particularly important to be honest at these times?

Understanding

The help-giver must walk a narrow line between gathering all the information necessary to be as useful as possible to the family and inquiring into areas of family privacy that are not pertinent to the issues at hand. Effective help-giving requires an understanding of a family's concerns and interests, but not minute details about every aspect of the family's life. By restricting attention to what is important to families (needs, concerns, aspirations, etc.) information gathering becomes focused rather than all-inclusive.

Solutions

The effective help-giver will use his/her time with the family seeking solutions to problems with meeting needs or achieving goals. **Time spent determining who to blame for problems or looking for reasons why things are not as they ought to be does not contribute to meeting family needs.** The family's needs exist irrespective of who or what is the cause. Emphasis should be placed on solutions rather than causes.

Actions

The effective help-giver avoids spending time looking for causes, but instead focuses on identifying needs. In a similar fashion, he/she moves the family as rapidly as possible from identifying needs to determining what resources will meet these needs and what actions must be taken to obtain these resources. Negative, problem-oriented discussions are held to a minimum; positive exchanges provide results like these:

- help-giver listening promotes help-seeker sharing
- help-seeker sharing promotes help-giver understanding
- understanding promotes help-seeker/help-giver exploration
- exploration promotes <u>ACTION</u>

Confidentiality

Confidentiality must be maintained and preserved at all times. The help-giver must make absolutely clear to the family that what is shared during conversations or what is written onto forms will be held in strictest confidence. **If the help-giver desires to discuss any information about the family with others (e.g., team members), this request must be made explicitly clear to the family. And without the family's express permission, it must also be explicitly clear that no information will be shared with others .**

Can you count these practices among your regular methods for working with families? It would be a good habit for all help-givers to review these characteristics regularly; they are guaranteed to enhance your working relationship with families who are seeking help.

Roles for the Help-Giver

Families seeking help have many different needs which often require the help-giver to relate to them in a number of different roles. While these roles are not mutually exclusive, it is useful to distinguish among them. Some are illustrated in the dialogue below.

Mother: I have to go back to work full time in order to keep health insurance for the three of us, and also just to help keep the monthly bills paid. I am so worried about finding a baby-sitter, though.

Help-giver: What kind of child care arrangement would you like to have? Day care? A private sitter?

Mother: I'd really like to find someone in a good home who'd keep the baby there, but I guess since I don't know anyone and have such little time until I start back to work, I'll have to settle for whatever I can find.

Help-giver: I can tell you're really anxious about this, but I'm not sure you'll have to settle for just anyone. Let's talk about some ways you might go about finding a sitter.

Since you'd most like to have child care in an individual home, let's start by looking at some ways you might find this type of help. Do you have any friends or neighbors or relatives who use this type of child care or who might know of someone who does? What about some of the people you work with who have children?

Mother: Actually, my sister-in-law has a sitter who keeps her son part time, and Judy, my friend at work, takes her children to the home of someone she speaks of very highly.

Help-giver: So, now you have two people who have found just the situation you're looking for. Can you check with them for the names and telephone numbers of their sitters? They might even know of other possibilities for child care.

Mother: Yes, I guess so. But how will I know if I can trust any sitter with my baby?

Help-giver: I know it's going to be very difficult for you to leave your baby in someone else's care since you've been her primary care provider since birth. It'll be an adjustment for both of you.

Mother: You can't imagine how I've agonized over this. I have looked at our budget over and over and I just can't come up with a way for us to manage without my salary and insurance.

Help-giver: It's true that it will be difficult for you to separate from the baby, but there are some things you can do to help choose a sitter you can have confidence in from the beginning.

Mother: I certainly want to have a good talk with anyone I'm considering, and in her home, too, where I can get a feel for the place. I really hope I'll get several recommendations for care from my friends or family, but I can't just take someone else's word on a sitter.

Help-giver: That's definitely a good idea. You might even want to get references from other parents who have used the sitters you're considering. Have you given any thought to specifically what you're going to look for or ask when you visit potential sitters?

Mother: I know I want a place that's clean and safe for children. I also want someone who will love her and spend time with her, not leave her lying in a crib.

Help-giver: I agree with both those points. You might want to spend some time thinking about other requirements and questions, and then write them down and take with you. That way you can be sure to ask all the important questions to each person you visit. I have a brochure at the office I'll send you; it might give you ideas for other questions.

I notice you haven't mentioned your baby's need for tube feeding. Have you thought how you will talk to potential sitters about this?

Mother: I'm afraid that might be the most difficult part. It's so scary to most people who aren't familiar with her. Yet I'm so accustomed to it, I hardly even give it a thought.

Help-giver: You certainly have done well with the feedings. You might want to think back on what it was like for you in the beginning, though, and recall the little "tricks" and routines you learned over time to make the feedings go more smoothly. You can use this information when you're teaching someone else. I'm sure your positive attitude toward tube feeding will be very convincing.

Mother: You know you're right! I taught both her daddy and her grandmother to feed her, and they're both almost as good as I am.

Help-giver: I've noticed what a genuine interest your husband takes in caring for the baby, and how comfortable he's become feeding her. Will he be involved in helping to find a sitter?

Mother: I'm sure he'd go with me if I asked him. So far, I really haven't had a plan, so I haven't known what to ask for. Actually, he'd be a big help in this since he often sees things a bit differently than I do. And I won't feel all the responsibility for making such a big decision.

Help-giver: I think that together the two of you will handle the challenge of finding an appropriate sitter quite well. You already have several people to contact for names, some ideas on your expectations of a sitter, and confidence in your ability to teach someone to give tube feedings.

I'll send the brochure I promised and call in a couple of days to see how you're progressing in finding a sitter for your baby.

❖❖❖❖❖

The ease and understanding with which the help-giver can move into and out of these roles as necessary will contribute to the process of enabling and empowering families. Let's look at these roles in more detail.

Empathic Listener

Two of the most important tools available to the help-giver are the ability to really hear what people are trying to say and the skill of communicating this understanding back to the speaker. We name these abilities active and reflective listening. An empathic listener (help-giver) uses these strategies to encourage family members to express their concerns about the family and individual family members and to reassure the speaker that she/he has been heard correctly.

ACTIVE LISTENING. An active listener shows interest and concern about what is important to the family and elicits the feelings and perceptions of different family members. Interest and concern are communicated both verbally and non-verbally to the family.

elicit feelings

For instance, "You seem very concerned about your child's future. What types of things worry you?" demonstrates active listening, an empathic verbal response. Nodding one's head, maintaining eye contact, and leaning toward the speaker are examples of empathic non-verbal communication.

REFLECTIVE LISTENING. An active listener primarily elicits information and feelings from the speaker. A reflective listener, on the other hand, helps the speaker clarify the meaning of his/her statements -- and more importantly, his/her feelings. A reflective listener may also point out changes in the speaker's tone or speech patterns that could provide insight when clarified.

helps to clarify meaning of statements

restate / rephrase.

Reflective listening is illustrated in these three exchanges:

Speaker: I feel so down about working things out with my wife."

Help-giver: I don't quite understand what you mean by "down?" Could you tell me what "down" means to you?

❖ ❖ ❖ ❖ ❖

Speaker: I'm really nervous about this job interview on Monday.

Help-giver: Does that mean you're worried the interview won't go well? Or is there something else about the job that concerns you?

❖ ❖ ❖ ❖ ❖

Speaker: Sometimes when I think about my child's future ...

Help-giver: I notice you didn't even finish your sentence, and your voice seems so weak, almost like a frightened child. Are you frightened about what the future holds for your child? and for you?

A reflective listener restates or rephrases what a family member says to help clarify exactly what is meant by his/her statements. A reflective response should always be worded in such a way as to invite the family member to agree with or correct the help-giver's understanding of the original statement.

Remember what your role is.

Practicing your empathic listening skills is extremely important to the establishment and strengthening of the partnership between help-seeker and help-giver. **However, it should always be kept in mind that when the complexities of the family's emotional needs are beyond the competencies of the help giver, it is most necessary to assist the family in finding professional counseling.**

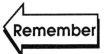

Remember

Teacher/Therapist

The role that help-givers are called upon most often to assume when working with families of small children is that of teacher or therapist. Often the help-giver must also prepare parents to function in these capacities with their child. This is an important role for several reasons, such as:

- allowing parents to be the ones to meet their child's needs, and so become more self-reliant

- increasing family interdependency

- enhancing or developing the child's competence thus permitting him/her to become a more socially adaptive member of the family.

Incorporating Child-Level Interventions into Daily Routines

Calling upon parents to act as teachers/therapists for their children can add considerably to the stress and demands of their days. In order to minimize these negative outcomes, it is crucial that child-level interventions be incorporated into the daily routines for the family as often as possible. When this blending of routines and interventions is successful, the efforts promote rather than interfere with family functioning.

The role of the help-giver is to assist parents in finding ways of incorporating interventions and therapy into normal daily activities, rather than asking families to set aside large amounts of time for teaching. Only by knowing the strengths of the family and of the child will the help-giver have the necessary information to suggest ways of addressing the needs of both.

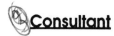 Consultant

The help-giver who functions as a consultant provides information and opinions *in response* to requests made by families and their network members. Frequently, a family does not realize or understand all the implications of their own situation.

For example, a relative or a neighbor may be reluctant or unwilling to help the family with their handicapped child because they have no knowledge or experience with a child in that condition. It is not that these informal support network members do not want to help, but that they feel incapable of helping.

In the role of consultant, the help-giver provides information that the family requests in order to to make more informed decisions and information that others can use to be better sources of support to the family.

Can you recall the first experience you had working with a handicapped child?

What concerns or fears are common for anyone in that position?

Resource

Families often are not aware of which services exist in the community that could be useful to them because they have had no previous need for these services. One of the very important roles that the help-giver can assume is that of providing information about community resources and services to the family. In this capacity, the help-giver becomes a "clearinghouse" for community information which helps families discover ways to meet their own needs.

Enabler

Often it is not enough to simply make a family aware of available community services and programs if they lack the skills and experience necessary to take advantage of these resources. When the help-giver functions as an enabler, he/she works with the family to assist them in accessing these resources.

Critical to performing this role in a way that empowers and strengthens families is to remember that the family should be enabled to take action for themselves, rather than the help-giver acting for them. For example, rather than the help-giver providing transportation for a family to visit a certain program, he/she could help the family work out a plan for seeking transportation from other possible sources.

Mobilizer

As a mobilizer, the help-giver links the family with others (individuals or groups) who can provide new or alternative perspectives on ways to go about meeting needs. This expands the pool of potential assistance to the family beyond the resources the help-giver has access to and beyond those provided by the community of which the help-giver is aware.

Part of the process of helping a family involves identifying people in their own social support network (relatives, friends, neighbors, employers, clergy, etc.) who may be used as a source of aid and assistance. As a mobilizer of support network members, the help-giver works to bring together the "key players" in this network and the family in need.

Mediator

Sometimes a family will have had many negative encounters with members of their informal or formal support networks. When this has occurred, it may be necessary for the help-giver to structure some future meetings between the family and representatives from these networks in an attempt to re-establish a more cooperative working relationship. The primary purpose of these encounters is to create a mood and set expectations for additional positive, task-oriented, and mutually reinforcing exchanges between the family and these network members.

 **Mediating exchanges between the family and other formal and informal sources of support (agencies or individuals) is a function that should be performed by the help-giver for a limited time -- only long enough for the family to begin negotiating with others and meeting their own needs.**

Advocate

As an advocate, the help-giver works on behalf of families and teaches families to work in their own best interests to:

- protect their rights as parents as well as the rights of their children,

- negotiate effectively with policy-makers on issues of concern to them, and

- create opportunities to influence the establishment of new policies on behalf of children and families in similar situations.

The families, the help-giver, policy makers, and policy enforcers should share responsibility for developing and providing services to families.

You should now be familiar with the characteristics which distinguish an effective help-giver/help-seeker relationship and with some of the key roles help-givers are called upon to play in their work with families.

After you complete the activities on the following pages, we'll consider some specific guidelines about providing help to families in a way that promotes positive family functioning.

How many roles did the help-giver in the preceding dialogue display?

Which of these roles do you assume most often? Are there any you don't feel comfortable assuming? What can you do to lessen your discomfort?

Stop and Practice Your Skills

Activity: Help-Giver/Help-Seeker Matrix

On the preceding pages we have explored a number of roles played by the help-giver, some of which relate to identifying and clarifying the feelings of a family member. This can be a very powerful process for many people to experience.

One of the best ways to remind ourselves of the power and importance of that experience is to recall times when we have both helped and been helped by others and how those experiences made us feel.

On the following page is a matrix for you to complete. Select situations from your past that were significant at the time and list your thoughts and feelings and the related behaviors or actions in each cell of the matrix. Then answer the questions below.

Questions

- How did it feel to be in each of the different roles represented on the matrix?
- In which situation(s) were your feelings the strongest? Why?
- How easy was it for you to remember your feelings?
- Are you often aware of your own feelings when working with families?

Help-Giver/Help-Seeker Matrix

THINK OF A SITUATION...

When someone helped me and there was a <u>positive</u> outcome I felt: What had the other person done?	When someone helped me and there was a <u>negative</u> outcome I felt: What had the other person done?
When I helped someone and there was a <u>positive</u> outcome, the other person said or did this: What had you done?	When I helped someone and there was a <u>negative</u> outcome, the other person said or did this: What had you done?

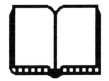

Tips From the Text

Characteristics of Effective Help-Seeker and Help-Giver Exchanges

- The help-giver must establish a <u>relationship</u> with the family which develops into a partnership built on mutual trust.

- <u>Communication</u> should demonstrate the help-giver's respect for all family members; use active and reflective listening skills.

- Being <u>honest</u> and up-front ensures strong relationships and good communication.

- <u>Understanding</u> must be focused on the family's needs and interests.

- Emphasis should be placed on <u>solutions</u>, not causes or blame.

- Solutions should be quickly translated into <u>actions</u> rather than dwelling on the concerns and problems.

- <u>Confidentiality</u> is essential -- it must be maintained and preserved at all times.

Roles of the Help-Giver

- **EMPATHIC LISTENER.** Encourages family members to express needs and concerns and clarifies what is said (using active and reflective listening skills).

- **TEACHER/THERAPIST.** Prepares parents to assume an instructional role with their child, then teaches the parents how to incorporate child-level interventions into daily routines.

- **CONSULTANT.** Provides information and opinions requested by the family and by members of the family's informal support network.

- **RESOURCE.** Makes the family aware of services and community resources available to them.

- **ENABLER.** Helps the family access the available services and resources.

- **MOBILIZER.** Links the family with others who may provide alternative resources for meeting needs.

- **MEDIATOR.** Promotes positive cooperation in situations where many negative encounters have occurred previously.

- **ADVOCATE.** Helps families protect their rights, negotiate with policy-makers, and influence the establishment of new policies.

Responsibilities of the Help-Seeker and Help-Giver

In the second section of this manual, **Working with Families**, we discussed the responsibilities of the help-seeker (family) and of the help-giver in the type of partnership for growth presented in this training. This effort involves encouraging behaviors that will increase interdependence among family members and other support systems as well as promoting positive functioning within the family.

Let's summarize the roles of both parties below.

Help-Seekers:

• play the major role in deciding the needs/goals on which to focus

• decide which options (resources) will be chosen to meet their needs or achieve their goals

• take the necessary actions to carry out their plans

• in summary, are the essential agents of change

Help-Giver:

• has a positive approach and is a skilled listener

• recognizes and acknowledges family strengths and capabilities

• supports, encourages, and creates opportunities for growth and the development of additional competencies

These efforts are carried out in a spirit of cooperation and partnership that emphasizes joint responsibility between the help-seeker and the help-giver. **The goal of the model presented in this training manual is to assist help-seekers become better able to cope effectively with future needs and better able to effectively achieve future goals, but not to guarantee help-seekers a future without challenges or problems.**

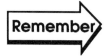

What experiences have you had forming partnerships with families?

How did you encourage their active participation?

The phenomenon of help-seeking and help-giving is a complex psychological and psychosocial event. When considered in the context of a discussion of needs, resources, and support, there is one major implication which help-givers should always keep in mind.

It is not just an issue of whether or not needs are met, but rather the ways in which support is provided and resources are acquired that determines whether or not families become enabled and empowered. Remember To become enabled and empowered, families must be actively involved in the process of identifying and mobilizing resources to meet their needs, and the help-giver must derive gratification and enjoyment from seeing others become capable and self-sufficient.

When help-seekers see themselves as singularly responsible for rescuing families, then the true needs of families are not being met.

Consequences of Help-Giving Interventions

Both the help-seeking literature in general (Fisher, Nadler & De Paulo, 1983) and that pertaining to handicapped children and their families specifically (Dunst & Trivette, 1988) provide information about types of help-giving behaviors that are likely to have either positive or negative consequences for help-seekers.

According to Fisher, Nadler, and Whitcher-Alagna (1983), behaviors on the part of help-givers that are likely to evoke positive, non-defensive reactions on the part of help-seekers include:

- positive help-giver attributions toward the help-seeker,
- help-giving that limits threats to the autonomy and self-esteem of the help-seeker, and
- help-giving that is accomplished in a cooperative manner.

In contrast, help-giving behaviors that are likely to evoke negative, defensive reactions include such things as:

- negative help-giver attributions toward the help-seeker,
- threats to help-seeker autonomy,
- paternalism, and
- help that restricts the freedom of the help-seeker to make his or her own choices.

While the outcomes of the behaviors described above may seem obvious, in practice it is sometimes difficult to keep in mind all the attributes of positive help-giving interventions. The next part of this section will provide you with specific guidelines you can use when engaged in help-giving interventions that are based on the model presented in this training.

Guidelines for Help-Giving Interventions

There is often tension or conflict between helping models commonly employed by professionals and the beliefs, attitudes, and behaviors that are necessary to foster greater involvement and responsibility on the part of parents for the care of their handicapped children.

loss of identity

Often help-givers feel threatened with a loss of importance or competence as families take a more active and responsible role in their own care. The model presented here supports parents by strengthening their decision-making rights and capabilities, and likewise supports help-givers by expanding the legitimate roles of help-givers necessary to support and strengthen family functioning.

Below are guidelines, organized into three clusters, that are considered to be determinants of the help-seeker's sense of control and self-esteem, which in turn influence the physical and psychological well-being of the whole family.

These guidelines were synthesized from an extensive review of the literature on help-giving and help-seeking exchanges by the authors of the accompanying text. (For more information, see pages 94-97 of the text. See the article by Dunst, Trivette, Davis, and Cornwell in <u>Children's Health Care</u>, 1988, for an elaboration on the guidelines which follow.)

ATTITUDES, BELIEFS, AND BEHAVIORS OF HELP-GIVERS ASSOCIATED WITH POSITIVE OUTCOMES IN HELP-GIVER/HELP-SEEKER EXCHANGES

Prehelping Attitudes and Beliefs

- Remember that help is most useful and effective when the approach of the help-giver is positive and supportive.
- Adopt helping models and behaviors that focus on the development of competencies that allow help-seekers to meet needs and solve problems.
- Assume that help-seekers are competent, or have the ability to become so, when it comes to managing the challenges and events in their lives.
- Strengthen individual and family functioning by building upon existing strengths rather than focusing on correcting deficits or assigning blame.
- Assume a proactive rather than reactive approach toward helping relationships.
- Assist families in becoming more capable and competent by promoting their strengths and abilities rather than focusing on prevention or treatment strategies.

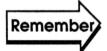

These attitudes and beliefs are the basis for an enabling model of helping, wherein help-givers provide opportunities and support for the acquisition of needed competencies by help-seekers.

Helping Behaviors

- Use active and reflective listening skills to aid in your understanding of help-seekers' concerns and needs.
- Help the family clarify their needs, concerns, and aspirations.
- Remember that help offered in response to family-identified needs is more favorably received than help that must be requested.
- Offer help that is compatible with the family's cultural and social norms.
- Offer help that is responsive to the family's own appraisal of its needs and concerns.
- Promote the family's increased knowledge, capabilities, and independence by offering help in a way that is competency producing.
- Employ help-seeker/help-giver partnerships as the mechanism for meeting needs and achieving aspirations in order to promote individual and family growth.
- Allow the locus of decision-making to rest clearly and completely with the family, including the decision to reject certain types of help when offered without jeopardizing future opportunities for help-seeker/help-giver exchanges.

This style of helping emphasizes genuine understanding and support of the needs and concerns of help-seekers and promotion of the skills and capabilities which allow help-seekers to increase control and determination of their lives.

Posthelping Responses and Consequences

- Accept and support the decisions of help-seekers, even when they differ from the decisions you as a help-giver might have made.
- Minimize the help-seeker's sense of indebtedness to the help-giver by being clear with yourself and the family that you are doing your job in a compassionate way, but not assuming the burden of responsibility for the family's well-being.
- Permit reciprocity in help-seeker/help-giver exchanges (e.g., informational or emotional) without creating any obligation for repayment.
- Minimize the psychological response costs of accepting help from the help-giver by offering help that reduces threats to self-esteem, moderates obligations to pay, protects the help-seeker's decision-making power, and promotes competence.
- Promote the help-seeker's belief in him- or herself as the agent responsible for making change in order to increase the chances that gains made will last over time.
- Maintain confidentiality at all times; share information about the family with others only with the family's express permission.

These responses to help-giving exchanges will have positive effects on the family's reaction to aid and whether changes made will last by ensuring that help-givers and help-giving acts are empowering rather than usurping.

Effective Help-Giving: A Summary

It is not uncommon for helping professionals to assume an approach that could be described as "rushing in and fixing" children and/or families in need without considering the consequences of their help-giving behaviors. Taking control and supplying needed resources may appear to be an effective way of meeting the needs of families with handicapped children; however, unless life-threatening conditions exist, this approach does nothing to build the necessary competence and confidence which would allow families to manage their children's health care needs independently.

Increasing family knowledge, building family competencies, and enhancing family independence does not mean a diminishing of the help-giver's role. On the contrary, the help-giver's legitimate role is expanded to include the special knowledge and behaviors necessary to effectively enable and empower the family.

Helping professionals who are willing to practice and persist in the model presented in this training will become increasingly comfortable employing enabling and empowering principles and behaviors. Their reward will be the satisfaction of seeing families become more active and capable in the care of their children.

Stop and Practice Your Skills

Activity: Enabling and Empowering Families

You have just had an opportunity to review guidelines for help-giving exchanges which, if followed, should enable and empower families in their efforts to identify and mobilize necessary resources for meeting their own needs.

Think back on your own experiences working with families and recall specific times when you followed one or more of the guidelines just presented. How did adhering to the guideline(s) affect the helping relationship? the family? Can you recall instances when you failed to follow any of these guidelines? What were the results?

Use the space on the next page to note two instances when you used these guidelines in working with families and two instances when you did not. Briefly state the consequences in each case and which particular guidelines were involved. (Since reading this manual, would you carry out these interventions differently if they were to recur?)

GUIDELINES FOLLOWED

Case #1:

Consequences:

Guidelines Involved:

Case #2:

Consequences:

Guidelines Involved:

GUIDELINES NOT FOLLOWED

Case #3:

Consequences:

Guidelines Involved:

Case #4:

Consequences:

Guidelines Involved:

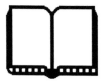

Tips From the Text

Responsibilities of Help-Seekers and Help-Givers

Help-Seekers:

- play the major role in deciding on which needs or goals to focus
- decide which options (resources) will be chosen to meet their needs or achieve their goals
- take the necessary actions to carry out their plans
- in summary, are the essential agents of change

Help-Givers:

- have a positive approach and are skilled listeners
- recognize and acknowledge family strengths and capabilities
- support, encourage, and create opportunities for growth and the development of additional competencies

Consequences of Help-Giving

Positive consequences to help-giving interventions result from:

- positive help-giver attributions toward the help-seeker
- help-giving that limits threats to the autonomy and self-esteem of the help-seeker
- help-giving that is accomplished in a cooperative manner

Negative consequences to help-giving interventions result from:

- negative help-giver attributions toward the help-seeker
- threats to help-seeker autonomy
- paternalism
- help that restricts the freedom of the help-seeker to make his or her own choices

Guidelines for Help-Giving Interventions

Help is more effective and more favorably received when:

- the attitude of the help-giver is positive and supportive

- it focuses on the development of help-seeker competencies for meeting needs and solving problems
- the help-seeker is assumed to be competent or capable of developing needed competencies
- emphasis is on building upon existing strengths rather than correcting deficits
- a proactive rather than reactive approach is taken toward helping relationships
- focus is on promoting strengths and abilities rather than on prevention or treatment strategies
- active and reflective listening skills are adopted to help understand help-seekers' concerns and needs
- family needs, concerns, and aspirations are first clarified
- it is offered in response to family-identified needs rather than having to be requested
- the help-giver does not imply that the family's needs are different from needs of other normal families
- it is an appropriate response to the specific need or concern of the family
- it increases the knowledge, capabilities and independence of the family or individual family members
- it is the result of joint efforts -- a partnership between the help-giver and the family -- which can promote further responsibility and efforts on the family's part
- the locus of decision-making remains with the family, including the right to refuse help without penalty
- the decisions of the help-seekers are supported by the help-giver
- it minimizes the sense of indebtedness felt by the help-seeker
- the possibility of repayment or reciprocation exists but is not expected
- the real and perceived costs of seeking help do not outweigh the benefits
- the family sees improvement (needs being met) and consider themselves to be responsible for making and maintaining the change
- confidentiality is scrupulously maintained at all times

Writing Family Support Plans

Trainer's Notes

Writing Family Support Plans builds upon the previous five sections by taking a close look at the form used for Individualized Family Support Plans.

Time

For a training group of 10 people, allow 1 hour to discuss this section and answer questions.

Materials

For this session you will need to have:

- training manual for *Developing Individualized Family Support Plans*

- *Enabling and Empowering Families* (Dunst, Trivette & Deal, 1988)

- chalkboard and chalk or newsprint and markers, along with masking tape to attach pieces of newsprint to the wall

- optional: overheads (4 pages) of IFSP

- optional: overhead projector and screen or expanse of light-colored wall

Before You Begin

- Be certain that equipment is available and that both equipment and seating are arranged properly.

- Read the material in the training manual.

- Practice filling out the forms so that you can answer questions.

- Be prepared to discuss the questions below.

 **Discussion Questions**

❑ *What differences do you see between the IFSP as described by Public Law 99-457 and the Individualized Family Support Plan proposed in this manual?*

❏ The content of the Family Support Plan attempts to accurately and sufficiently reflect the goals of this family-based assessment and intervention model. *Is there additional information you think would be necessary to capture during a family assessment?*

❏ The table of the 7-point scale shows the recommended rating scale to be used with the Family Support Plan for evaluating efforts to meet family needs. *Do you think this scale sufficiently represents the range of possible situations you will need to document? What are the benefits to having a simple and succinct rating scale?*

Tips for Leading Discussion

- Ask if there are any questions from the reading.

- Try to get other trainees to respond to these questions and issues from their own experiences.

- If trainees' experiences have not been positive, or if they lack experience in family-directed encounters, be sure to reinforce the attitudes and recommendations in these readings.

Activities

There are no activities in this section, but this section leads directly into the case studies and use of the forms presented in the next section of the manual.

Points to Look For

The five sections of this manual which precede this section have presented the philosophy behind and components of a family-based assessment and intervention model. In this section, the Individualized Family Support Plan which is derived from this model will be compared to the Individualized Family Service Plan as prescribed by Congress (P.L. 99-457 [Part H]) in terms of intent, focus on family enabling and development, and prognosis for success. After the comparison, you will see a detailed description of the actual form used in the Individualized Family Support Plan as developed by the FIPP. In the next section you will have an opportunity to see two completed Individualized Family Support Plans based on case studies.

Listed below are some important points to look for and remember as you read. You can use the back of this page to make your own notes or responses to the items below.

 **Discussion Questions**

❑ *What differences do you see between the IFSP as described by Public Law 99-457 and the Individualized Family Support Plan proposed in this manual?*

❑ The content of the Family Support Plan attempts to accurately and sufficiently reflect the goals of this family-based assessment and intervention model. *Is there additional information you think would be necessary to capture during a family assessment?*

❑ The table of the 7-point scale shows the recommended rating scale to be used with the Family Support Plan for evaluating efforts to meet family needs. *Do you think this scale sufficiently represents the range of possible situations you will need to document? What are the benefits to having a simple and succinct rating scale?*

Notes

WRITING FAMILY SUPPORT PLANS

Western Carolina Center
Family, Infant and Preschool Program
Individualized Family Support Plan

Successful implementation of a family-level intervention plan depends on a clear understanding of the model on which the plan is based. This information must be coupled, however, with the procedures described by recent legislation (PL-99-457) involving educational services for handicapped infants and pre-school children.

Overview of the Plan

The approach to family-level assessment and intervention described in the section of this manual entitled **Working With Families** is based upon research (done at the Family, Infant and Preschool Program in Morganton, North Carolina), which suggests methods to make family-level intervention practices both enabling and empowering. Public Law 99-457 (The Reauthorization of the Education for All Handicapped Children Act) supports these research findings by describing specific measures to be used in family-level interventions. One major component of this law is an early intervention program establishing family systems services for handicapped and at-risk infants and toddlers. A major requirement of the early intervention initiative is the Individualized Family Service Plan.

This section briefly describes the required content of the Individualized Family Service Plan, then presents a critique of the plan, with emphasis on the logic upon which it is based. Following this critique, a more functional approach to developing family-level intervention plans is proposed. This alternative approach is based on the research findings from the FIPP and the principles described earlier in this manual.

Please note that this section repeats a description of the required components of the IFSP, previously presented in an earlier section of this manual, in order to make a clear comparison between the IFSP as described in Public Law 99-457 and the more functional and flexible approach to developing family-level intervention plans suggested by the FIPP.

Think About It...

Are you beginning to see any parallels between the model which was presented in the last 5 sections and the Public Law 99-457?

The Individualized Family Service Plan

One of the requirements of the Early Intervention Program initiative of the recently enacted P.L. 99-457 (Part H) is the Individualized Family Service Plan (IFSP). According to the *Congressional Record* (1986, p.H7895), the IFSP must contain:

1. a statement of the child's present levels of development (cognitive, speech/language, psychosocial, motor, and self-help)

2. a statement of the family's strengths and needs relating to enhancing the child's development

3. a statement of major outcomes expected to be achieved for the child and family and the criteria, procedures, and timelines for determining progress

4. the specific early intervention services necessary to meet the unique needs of the child and family

5. the projected dates for the initiation of services and expected duration

6. the name of the case manager who will be responsible for the implementation of the plan

7. procedures for transition from early intervention into a preschool program

The IFSP is similar to the Individualized Education Plan (IEP) required as part of P.L. 94-142. The research staff at the FIPP have experimented over the past six years with different formats for developing and implementing family-level intervention plans (including the IFSP proposed by PL 99-457). This research has found that the approach to formulating family plans described as part of the IFSP requirements often does not work very well, may set the occasion for conflict between families and professionals, and may even have negative consequences. The IFSP is based upon logic and reasoning that make the utility of the plan, at least as proposed, highly questionable.

◆◆◆◆◆

<u>One of the presuppositions</u> upon which the IFSP is based is that it is possible (even desirable) to work out long-term intentions, methods, and procedures for meeting family-level needs. This assumption is not realistic because family needs change so rapidly, sometimes even daily. By the time long-term plans are formulated and put into writing, the needs have changed and the plan is no longer responsive to what the family considers important. Extensive experiences working with families and devising family-level intervention plans have led to the conclusion that it is very difficult to develop plans with long-range goals, methods, and outcomes which survive over an extended period of time.

A second presupposition of the IFSP involves a requirement that the plan contain a statement of the family's needs related to enhancing the child's development. This statement presumes that all families identify child-related concerns as needs and goals.

On the one hand, this requirement is unfounded because many families often have other needs that take precedence and consume their time and energy. Several studies have shown that family-identified child-related needs are related to needs in other areas, but the needs in other areas often must be addressed before child-related needs can be addressed.

On the other hand, this requirement presumes that there should be family-level needs related to the child's development regardless of whether the family views this to be the case. If this is implemented, it will likely encourage a defensive reaction from families, produce negative effects (e.g., increased stress), and potentially have other adverse consequences. Needs statements regarding a family's role in promoting the child's development should be made only to the extent that the family identifies this as an important concern. Otherwise, there will be increased risk of conflict and disagreement between the family and the professional.

❖❖❖❖❖

A third presupposition of the IFSP is the assumption that more is better. The IFSP must contain a statement about both the frequency and intensity of services to meet needs. This requirement suggests that frequency and intensity are major determinants of successful intervention efforts and ignores the fact that informal treatments can have, and in many cases have had, very powerful effects on family functioning (e.g., providing a parent with written information on the child's handicapping condition, which promotes knowledge of the disability and decreases stress associated with the unknown).

This requirement also assumes that needs are static and stable, an assumption that is generally unfounded. It is difficult to state with any accuracy the frequency and intensity at which services should be rendered to meet family needs when concerns and priorities change so rapidly. Needs are a relative, changing phenomenon, and interventions to meet needs must change accordingly.

❖❖❖❖❖

The fourth and most concerning aspect of the IFSP has to do with the role the "case manager" is expected to play in implementing the plan. According to the *Congressional Record* (1986), the IFSP must contain the "name of the case manager ... *who will be responsible for implementation of the plan and coordination with other agencies and persons* " [italics added] (p. H7895).

This requirement states that the case manager is responsible for securing resources to meet the family's needs. This directly threatens a family's ability to become competent because it removes control from the family rather than empowering them. This requirement of the IFSP violates many of the principles of helping relationships that are known to be both enabling and empowering (Dunst & Trivette, 1987). A case manager should not be responsible for implementing the plan. Rather, he or she should assume helping roles so that a family can be enabled and empowered to mobilize resources to meet needs.

This section has outlined some of the concerns about the IFSP. As already noted, attempts to develop and implement family-level intervention plans from a perspective similar to the IFSP were often found to be unresponsive to the changing needs of families. This led to a reconsideration of how family-level intervention plans should be conceptualized, implemented, and evaluated.

An Alternative Framework for Developing IFSP's

It is useful to distinguish between static and fluid family-level intervention plans as a basis for proposing a more flexible and functional approach to developing and implementing family-level interventions. A static plan does not permit, or discourages, frequent changes and modifications once goals, methods, and outcomes have been specified. In contrast, a fluid plan not only permits but encourages frequent modifications based on changes in a family's situations and conditions and thus is flexible and is more functional.

The system for writing and implementing the Individualized Family Support Plan as described in this manual is flexible and functional. The format encourages modifications in response to the changing needs, interests, and aspirations of families and family members. Still, it is important to note that the most important dynamic in working with families is positive interaction, not always what is on paper.

The Individualized Family Support Plan form is three pages long. It is suggested that a matrix be used in conjunction with the IFSP. A matrix is the way to integrate goals with the daily routines of the child and family by describing the daily routines during which the family can work on specific goals. The next section of this manual will give you the opportunity to practice filling out the Individualized Family Support Plan form and the matrix. First, let us look at the parts of these forms one page at a time in some detail.

(NOTE: A reduced version is shown here for reference only; a full-size version appears in the next section of this manual.)

The Individualized Family Support Plan Form

Western Carolina Center
Family, Infant and Preschool Program
Individualized Family Support Plan

Background Information:	Family Member's Name:	Relationship to Child:
Child's Name: _____		
Family's Name: _____		
No. OPD-0__: _____		
Date of Birth: _____ Age:		
County: _____		

Family Support Plan Team			
Name	Title	Agency	Date
	Parent		
	Case Coordinator		

Team Review Dates			
30 Days:	3 Months:	6 Months:	9 Months:

Page I has spaces to record:

- the child's name, age, date of birth and county of residence
- the family's name
- the names of immediate family members, their dates of birth and ages, and their relationships to the target child
- the name of the case coordinator (help-giver) who will function in a number of capacities to enable and empower families
- the names of other people who will be involved in the intervention

Child's Name _____ OPD.0 _____ Family's Name _____

CHILD'S FUNCTIONING LEVEL								
Domain	CA	Age Level/Range	Domain	CA	Age Level/Range	Domain	CA	Age Level/Range

CHILD'S STRENGTHS	FAMILY'S STRENGTHS

RESOURCES AND SUPPORT SERVICES	Dates		RESOURCES AND SUPPORT SERVICES	Dates	
	Started	Ended		Started	Ended

Page 2 has spaces to record:

- the child's current levels of functioning according to developmental domain, age level, and age range
- the child's major strengths
- family strengths as a part of family functioning style
- informal and formal services (types of family/child involvement) that are to be used by the family and the dates these services are started and ended

Family and child involvement might include such varied things as parent support groups, the child's enrollment in a preschool classroom, physical or speech therapy for the child, parent participation in a training program, or any other type of involvement *specifically* chosen to meet one or more family-identified needs.

Name _____ OPD.0_____ Family's Name _____ IFSP# _____
FIPP Staff Member _____

Date / #	NEED/PROJECT OUTCOME STATEMENT	SOURCE OF SUPPORT/ RESOURCE	COURSE OF ACTION	FAMILY'S EVALUATION	
				Date	Rating

Family's Evaluations:
1...Situation changed, no longer a need
2...Situation unchanged, still a need, goal or project
3...Implementation begun, still a need, goal or project
4...Outcome partially attained or accomplished
5...Outcome accomplished or attained, but not to the family's satisfaction
6...Outcome mostly accomplished or attained to the family's satisfaction
7...Outcome completely accomplished or attained to the family's satisfaction

Page 3 has spaces to record:

- the child's name, family's name, the name of the case coordinator, and the page number of the cumulative record of the Individualized Family Support Plan

- each family need and project as it is identified, the dates on which the needs and projects were identified, and at least a rough rank-order number for the needs

  Needs should be stated in an "in order to" format so that the purpose of procuring a resource is as clear as possible. For example, a mother's need for information about her child's handicapping condition might be stated as follows: "Mother will obtain materials about X syndrome in order to become more knowledgeable about Johnny's condition."

- the specific resources that will be procured to meet the family's need and the source of support for the resources. This need not include anything more than a brief statement or list of support sources and resources that will be mobilized

- actions that will be taken to mobilize the resources necessary for meeting needs, stated succinctly in terms of what will be done and who will be responsible for accomplishing and carrying out the actions
- an evaluation, using the following 7-point scale, of the extent to which needs are met as a result of actions designed to mobilize resources

The case coordinator should add additional copies of page 3 as other family needs are identified. The case coordinator need only number the additional pages sequentially to have a cumulative record of work with the family.

The Seven-Point Scale

Rating Scale	Criteria
1	Situation changed, no longer a need
2	Situation unchanged, still a need, goal, or project
3	Implementation begun, still a need, goal, or project
4	Outcome partially attained or accomplished, but not to the family's satisfaction
5	Outcome accomplished or attained, but not to the family's satisfaction
6	Outcome mostly accomplished or attained to the family's satisfaction
7	Outcome completely accomplished or attained to the family's satisfaction

The Routines Matrix Form

Child's Name	OPD.0	Matrix #:

DATE STARTED	OBJECTIVES	ROUTINES						DATE ATTAINED

The routines matrix has spaces to record:

- the family's objectives for the child
- the date the family started working toward each objective
- the daily routines (such as meal time, bath time, etc.) into which each objective can be integrated
- the date each objective is attained to the family's satisfaction

Can you see how the Individualized Family Support Plan proposed here is flexible and functional?

Additional Features

The recommended rating scale for evaluating efforts to meet family needs is included on the third page of the Individualized Family Support Plan. When the case coordinator has contact with the family, he or she simply records the date of contact, assesses the extent to which the need is still present, and determines whether the need has been met or the goal or project has been achieved.

The simple format of the Individualized Family Support Plan provides an efficient system for identifying and meeting family needs. The simplicity of the plan allows case coordinators to spend more time employing help-giving behavior that enables and empowers families rather than filling out unnecessary paperwork.

This approach for identifying and meeting family needs represents at least one viable system for developing, implementing, and evaluating Individualized Family Support Plans. To be effective in work with families, one must be both flexible and functional in the ways in which one assesses needs and intervenes to meet them. Individualized Family Support Plans must be flexible and functional if help-givers are to be responsive to changes in the family system.

Tips From the Text

Critique of the IFSP as described by PL 99-457

- The statement of goals for extended periods of time is not realistic because families are affected by external events as well as internal changes, and their needs will change with these influences.

- Family needs may or may not be directly related to their handicapped child. It is important to allow the family to define their own needs and not limit them to needs directly related to the child.

- It is generally impossible to state with any accuracy the frequency and intensity at which services should be provided to meet family needs because concerns and priorities change so rapidly.

- The case manager should <u>not</u> be the main person responsible for implementing the family services plan. This responsibility should lie with the family, increasing their ability to become competent in meeting their own needs.

The FIPP Individualized Family Support Plan Alternative

- The Individualized Family Support Plan is flexible and functional.

- The Individualized Family Support Plan encourages frequent modifications in response to the changing needs, interests, and aspirations of families and individual family members.

- With the Individualized Family Support Plan, needs statements regarding a family's role in promoting the child's development are made only if the family identifies these as important concerns.

- The Individualized Family Support Plan rating scale is succinct.

- The scale offers enough options to accurately classify family progress in meeting needs and achieving goals.

- The simplicity of the scale increases the likelihood that evaluation of progress will take place whenever the opportunity occurs.

- The statements which accompany the scale do not judge whether the family is "progressing correctly" or "failing to progress," but only whether or not the family is still working on a project or goal or satisfied with an outcome.

Case Studies

Case Studies

Every family is unique, therefore an IFSP for any given family will look different from any other. The following case studies are only examples. They are unique to the families for whom they were written. These case studies are included as examples only; they are not models for other IFSP's.

It is difficult and not necessary to capture everything about a family on a form. Some of the interaction between the case coordinator and a family will not be written on the IFSP form. Also, note that the case study IFSP's contain many child-level as well as family-level goals. This also will vary according to individual families. Even IFSP's which contain more child-level goals than family-level goals will contribute to positive family interaction and a sense of accomplishment.

Example of Parts of the IFSP

Date / #	NEED/PROJECT OUTCOME STATEMENT	SOURCE OF SUPPORT/ RESOURCE	COURSE OF ACTION
9-8 / 1	Ricky will learn to cruise in order to develop independent walking.	Denise - will provide information on motor skills to parents and Ashley Ashley - will model activities Parents and grandparents - will provide opportunities for cruising	Ashley will model motor activities for family on weekly home visits. Parents and grandparents will carry out suggestions at home. Denise will provide consultation.

Explanation of Parts of the IFSP

NEED/PROJECT OUTCOME STATEMENT

"Ricky will learn to cruise" -- reflects detailed goal in terms of child's current stage of development.
"in order to develop independent walking" -- is the general, long-range outcome expected over time.

SOURCE OF SUPPORT/RESOURCE

This section is for naming the people or agencies providing resources. The roles played by anyone or anything listed here need to be described in the Course of Action column. For example, "Ashley will model activities" is extended in the course of action by stating when she will model activities.

COURSE OF ACTION

This section highlights clearly who is doing what and how it will be accomplished. The "who, when, where and how" in this column should contribute to achieving the Needs/ Project Outcome Statement in the first column.

Case Study #1

Susan Smith has two young daughters, Ann who is three years old and Mary, 20 months old, who was diagnosed soon after birth with Down syndrome. Mary has been involved in home-based intervention since age 8 months. Being a single mom has been hard for Susan because she is concerned for her children's emotional and physical well-being and because she is the sole provider for her family's financial needs. The father of the two girls is not involved and he has no contact with Susan. His whereabouts are unknown. Susan is currently looking for a job. She is a high school graduate and has good typing skills. Susan is willing and eager to obtain a job.

Assessment results indicated Mary's functioning levels are:

Social adaptation	14 months
Gross motor	13 months
Personal-social	11 months
Fine motor	10 months
Hearing/speech	14 months
Performance	10 months

Mary has many strengths. She is alert and sociable. She enjoys being with people. Mary attends to sounds and voices. She has learned to communicate using a yes/no response. Mary exhibits a lot of initiative and enjoys exploring her environment through crawling. Mary has few medical complications as a result of Down Syndrome. She has a history of many ear infections.

It is important to Susan to keep her family together and to give Mary as normal a lifestyle as possible. Susan has the support of her mother, brother, and some friends and church members. She is close to her family and friends. Susan feels positive about her family and their potential for growth. She promotes this positiveness through good communication with her children. She is optimistic about their lives together as a family.

Organizations in which the Smiths are involved include: Department of Social Services, Supplemental Security Income (SSI), church, and the home-based early intervention program.

Susan has expressed various needs in regard to Mary's development. She would like Mary to learn to feed herself and to improve her communication and vocalization skills. Susan would also like Mary to improve her locomotion skills.

Western Carolina Center
Family, Infant and Preschool Program
Individualized Family Support Plan

Background Information:

Child's Name: __Mary__

Family's Name: __Smith__

No. OPD-0__;

Date of Birth: __12-26-87__   Age: __20 mo.__

County:_____

Family Member's Name: Relationship to Child:

Family Member's Name	Relationship to Child
Susan Smith	mother
Ann Smith	older sister

Family Support Plan Team

Name	Title	Agency	Date
Susan	Parent		
Jane Jones	Case Coordinator	Home Based Program	8-1-88
John Johnson	Speech Pathologist	Home Based Program	8-1-88
Linda Williams	Teacher	Home Based Program	8-1-88
Don Hunter	Psychologist	Home Based Program	8-1-88
Pat Bennett	Nurse	Public Health Department	8-1-88

Team Review Dates

30 Days: 9-1-89	3 Months: 11-3-89	6 Months: 2-2-90	9 Months: 5-4-90

Child's Name Mary Smith OPD.0 Family's Name Smith

CHILD'S FUNCTIONING LEVEL

Domain	CA	Age Level/Range	Domain	CA	Age Level/Range	Domain	CA	Age Level/Range
Social adaptation	20 mo.	14 months (10-16)	Fine motor	20 mo.	10 months (7-12)			
Gross motor	20 mo.	13 months (11-14)	Hearing/speech	20 mo.	14 months (12-16)			
Per-social	20 mo.	11 months (9-15)	Performance	20 mo.	10 months (8-10)			

CHILD'S STRENGTHS

She is alert and interacts a lot with people. She engages in smiling behavior. She attends to sounds and voices and uses several words (yes, no). She explores her environment through crawling and shows a lot of initiative.

FAMILY'S STRENGTHS

Commitment to staying together and helping Mary live as normal a life as possible. Communication between mother and children is good. Has wide informal support network with family and friends, has positive outlook on the situation.

RESOURCES AND SUPPORT SERVICES

	Dates	
	Started	Ended
Department of Social Services	8-1-88	3-89
SSI	8-1-88	
Home-based services	8-1-88	
Employment Security Commission	9-18-88	

RESOURCES AND SUPPORT SERVICES

	Dates	
	Started	Ended

Name __Mary__ OPD.0 _____ Family's Name _____ Smith _____ IFSP# _____ FIPP Staff Member _____ Jane Jones

Date / #	NEED/PROJECT OUTCOME STATEMENT	SOURCE OF SUPPORT/ RESOURCE	COURSE OF ACTION	FAMILY'S EVALUATION Date	Rating
9-1-89 1	Susan will obtain employment in order to adequately meet her financial responsibilities for herself and her two children.	case coordinator - support to mom Susan Susan's mother - babysitting Susan's brother - babysitting Employment Security Commission - employment possibilities	Susan will fill out the appropriate forms at Employment Security Commission to start the process of finding a job. She will familiarize herself with their process and be aware of what her responsibilities are. Susan will talk with her mother and brother about babysitting while she interviews for jobs. Susan will also continue to read the classified ads in the paper and follow through on any job leads she feels might pertain to her. During weekly home visits, the case coordinator will check with Susan about progress in looking for a job.	9-1-89 9-18-89 9-29-89 10-13-89 11-3-89	2 3 3 3 7
		—			
9-1-89 2	Susan will find a day care center in order to provide adequate supervision of her children enabling her to maintain a full-time job.	case coordinator - will act as consultant and resource to mom Chamber of Commerce - list of day care centers friends - names of day care centers church members - names of day care centers Dept. of Social Services - names of day care centers newspaper - names of day care centers Susan's mother - babysitting Susan's brother - babysitting	Susan will obtain a list of possible day care centers from friends, the Chamber of Commerce, church members, DSS, and the newspaper. Susan will find out information such as types and ages of children served, cost, hours open, and other general information. At weekly home visits, the case coordinator will share information about what to look for in day care centers. Susan will narrow her list down to her top three choices and visit these programs personally before coming to a final decision. Susan's mother and brother can babysit while Susan visits day care centers. Susan's children will then be enrolled in the chosen day care center.	9-1-89 9-18-89 9-29-89 10-13-89 11-3-89	2 3 2 4 7
	—				

Family's Evaluations:

1... Situation changed, no longer a need
2... Situation unchanged, still a need, goal or project
3... Implementation begun, still a need, goal or project
4... Outcome partially attained or accomplished
5... Outcome accomplished or attained, but not to the family's satisfaction
6... Outcome mostly accomplished or attained to the family's satisfaction
7... Outcome completely accomplished or attained to the family's satisfaction

| Name Mary | Family's Name _____ | OPD.0 | IFSP# _____ | FIPP Staff Member _____ Jane Jones | Smith |

Date / #	NEED/PROJECT OUTCOME STATEMENT	SOURCE OF SUPPORT/ RESOURCE	COURSE OF ACTION	FAMILY'S EVALUATION Date	Rating
9-1-89 / 3	Mary will locate food placed in front of her in order to learn to feed herself.	mom, family, friends case coordinator--will provide information on feeding strategies	Adults caring for Mary will place her in her high chair with a cracker on the tray at snacks and mealtimes. During weekly home visits, the case coordinator will present information on feeding and answer questions	9-1-89 9-18-89 9-29-89	2 3 3
9-1-89 / 4	Mary will make sounds when presented with familiar objects, sounds and smells to increase her communication abilities.	mom, family, friends case coordinator--will provide information on teaching strategies	Adults caring for Mary will talk with her about familiar objects, sounds and smells during everyday activities and reinforce her sounds, encourage Mary to repeat the name of the object, sound or smell. During weekly home visits, the case coordinator will present information on encouraging vocalizations.	9-1-89 9-29-89 10-13-89 11-3-89	2 3 3 3
9-1-89 / 5	Mary will find toys placed just out of her reach to begin exploring her environment.	mom, family, friends case coordinator--will provide information on teaching strategies	Mom will arrange an area at home for Mary with her toys, and adults caring for Mary will encourage her to find toys within this area. During weekly home visits, the case coordinator will present information on encouraging exploration.	9-1-89 9-18-89 9-29-89 11-3-89	2 2 3 7
9-1-89 / 6	Mary will make transitions from sitting to standing in order to eventually walk.	mom, family, friends case coordinator--will provide information on teaching strategies	Adults caring for Mary will place cushions on the floor and use a favorite toy to encourage her to climb on the cushions and pull to standing at the couch. During weekly home visits, the case coordinator will present information on motor development.	9-1-89 9-18-89 9-29-89 10-13-89 11-3-89	2 2 2 3 3

Family's Evaluations:
1... Situation changed, no longer a need
2... Situation unchanged, still a need, goal or project
3... Implementation begun, still a need, goal or project
4... Outcome partially attained or accomplished
5... Outcome accomplished or attained, but not to the family's satisfaction
6... Outcome mostly accomplished or attained to the family's satisfaction
7... Outcome completely accomplished or attained to the family's satisfaction

Name __Mary__ Family's Name __OPD.0__ IFSP# _____ FIPP Staff Member __Jane Jones__

Smith

Date	#	NEED/PROJECT OUTCOME STATEMENT	SOURCE OF SUPPORT/ RESOURCE	COURSE OF ACTION	FAMILY'S EVALUATION Date	Rating
9-29-89	7	Mary will bring finger foods to her mouth in order to learn to feed herself.	mom, family, friends case coordinator--will provide information on teaching strategies	Adults caring for Mary will provide finger foods and direct her through the motions of taking food to her mouth, as needed. During weekly home visits, the case coordinator will present information on feeding.	9-29-89 10-13-89 11-3-89	2 4 6
9-29-89	8	Mother will locate a pediatrician in town in order for Mary to have adequate routine medical care in her home community.	mom case coordinator--will provide information about medical resources in the community	During weekly home visits, the case coordinator will provide information on local pediatric services. Mom will make the call to get an appointment with the doctor of her choice.	9-29-89 10-13-89	2 7
11-15-89	9	Mary will attend the day care center in order to have experiences with non-handicapped peers.	case coordinator--consultation to day care staff	The case coordinator will provide consultation and information to the day care staff about Down Syndrome at least once a month.	11-15-89	2

Family's Evaluations:
1... Situation changed, no longer a need
2... Situation unchanged, still a need, goal or project
3... Implementation begun, still a need, goal or project
4... Outcome partially attained or accomplished
5... Outcome accomplished or attained, but not to the family's satisfaction
6... Outcome mostly accomplished or attained to the family's satisfaction
7... Outcome completely accomplished or attained to the family's satisfaction

Child's Name Mary Smith   OPD.0   Matrix #: 1

To go with 1 Goal?

DATE STARTED	OBJECTIVES	Mealtimes	Snacks	Playtime -- Morning	Playtime -- Afternoons	Playtime -- Evenings	Bathtime	DATE ATTAINED
				ROUTINES				
9-1-89	Mary will locate a cracker in front of her and bring it to her mouth.	X	X					
9-1-89	Mary will vocalize at the sound of her rattle. (Pair with the word "rattle.")			X	X	X	X	
9-1-89	Mary will vocalize when she smells bananas. (Pair with the word "banana.")	X	X					
9-1-89	Mary will find the "Happy Apple" when placed beyond her reach.			X	X	X	X	11-3-89
9-1-89	Mary will pull up to the cushions on the floor to get her "Happy Apple."			X	X	X		

Case Study #2

David and Alma Jones have one son, Ricky, who is 16 months old. Ricky was born prematurely with the complication of a patent (open) ductus in his heart. Ricky's early months at home were very difficult. He was physically weak with extremely low tone throughout his body. He would tire easily, but did not develop a regular sleep/wake pattern. He was extremely fussy and agitated -- a side effect of the heart medication.

Heart surgery was to be scheduled after Ricky's weight reached 12 pounds. Due to his low tone and heart problems, he had difficulty sucking and drinking more than 1 or 2 ounces at a time. At 4 weeks of age, a nasalgastro tube was inserted and Alma was instructed how to gaváge feed. By eight months, Ricky had finally gained the necessary weight and heart surgery was performed. A second surgery will be necessary around 5 years of age. He is no longer on medication.

Following his heart surgery, Ricky made tremendous gains. His endurance and color improved. He gained weight and could eat in a normal manner. He became a happy, curious, personable child. Ricky's pediatrician referred Ricky and his family to an early intervention program for help with gross motor and general developmental delays.

At 16 months, Ricky shows only minor delays in all developmental levels except for gross motor skills. Due to the continued low tone in his trunk and legs, his gross motor skills are more significantly delayed.

Assessment results indicated Ricky's functioning levels are:

Gross motor	8 months
Personal-social	13 months
Fine motor	13 months
Hearing/speech	13 months
Performance	15 months

Ricky has many strengths. For example, his curiosity and his tremendous personality combine to form wonderful social skills. Ricky has good intellectual ability and potential. His performance is due in part to his high motivational level. He possesses never-ending persistence, even though he still tires easily because of his heart problem.

The family is middle income. They see their strengths as being a family that is close and strong. David and Alma have much external support from Alma's parents, who provide emotional support to the family and childcare for Ricky.

David and Alma have expressed concerns about Ricky's inability to walk and his low muscle tone. They also question his lack of verbal communication. He will frequently gesture to communicate wants and needs rather than vocalizing. David and Alma are confused by his good receptive language skills, but lack of expressive ability. They also worry about Ricky not sleeping through the night. This also keeps them from having a full night's rest.

Western Carolina Center
Family, Infant and Preschool Program
Individualized Family Support Plan

Background Information:

Child's Name: Ricky Jones

Family's Name: Jones

No. OPD-0___:

Date of Birth: 3-15-88   Age: 19 mo.

County:

Family Member's Name:

Family Member's Name	Relationship to Child:
Alma	mother
David	dad

Family Support Plan Team

Name	Title	Agency	Date
Alma Jones	Parent		
David Jones	Parent		
Ashley Johnson	Case Coordinator	Early Intervention Program	9-10-89
Jackie Ward	Speech/Language Pathologist	Early Intervention Program	9-10-89
Don Marshall	Psychologist	Early Intervention Program	9-10-89
Judy Newton	Social Worker	Early Intervention Program	9-10-89
Linda Brown	Nurse	Early Intervention Program	9-10-89
Smith Nelson	Pediatrician	Early Intervention Program	9-10-89
Denise Bailey	Physical Therapist	Early Intervention Program	9-10-89

Team Review Dates

30 Days: 10-10-89	3 Months: 1-10-89	6 Months: 4-10-89	9 Months: 7-10-89

Child's Name Ricky Jones **OPD.0** **Family's Name** Jones

CHILD'S FUNCTIONING LEVEL

Domain	CA	Age Level/Range	Domain	CA	Age Level/Range
Gross motor	15.5	8 mo. /52	Eye/Hand	15.5	13 mo. /83
Per-social	15.5	13 mo. /83	Performance	15.5	15 mo. /97
Hearing/speech	15.5	13 mo. /83			G.Q. 79 / MA 12.3

CHILD'S STRENGTHS

Performance and intellectual abilities
Curiosity
Social skills
Personality
Motivation
Persistence

FAMILY'S STRENGTHS

Natural parenting
Family and extended family devotion to Ricky's progress
Toys provided
Both parents sharing in Ricky's care and nurture
Communication
Sense of humor

RESOURCES AND SUPPORT SERVICES

	Dates	
	Started	Ended
Early Intervention Program	9-10-89	
Church	ongoing	
Co-workers	ongoing	
Extended family	ongoing	

RESOURCES AND SUPPORT SERVICES

	Dates	
	Started	Ended
Private hospital	3-15-88	
Health department	ongoing	
PT consultant	9-13-89	
Private pediatrician	ongoing	

Name ___Ricky Jones___ OPD.0 ___ Family's Name ___Jones___ IFSP# ___ FIPP Staff Member ___Johnson___

Date #	NEED/PROJECT OUTCOME STATEMENT	SOURCE OF SUPPORT/ RESOURCE	COURSE OF ACTION	FAMILY'S EVALUATION Date	Rating
9-8 1	Alma and David will write down questions/concerns they have in order to plan Ricky's intervention planning day.	Ashley - will listen, provide support and information Grandparents - will contribute observations	Ashley will share grandparents' findings & observations of Ricky's development and give developmental checklist to parents. On weekly visits, Ashley will explain the team process . Parents will talk with grandparents, formulate concerns, and bring them in writing on intervention planning day. Ashley will develop schedule for the day	9-10-89 10-10-89	3 7
9-8 2	Family will obtain a physical therapy evaluation for Ricky in order to plan activities to encourage independent walking.	Denise - will assess motor skills Alma and David - will provide background information about Ricky's development	Parents will make an appointment with Denise and participate in the assessment. Denise will assess Ricky's current motor skills and provide verbal and written information to parents on weekly home visits.	9-13-89	6
9-8 3	Ricky will get from a prone position to a sitting position in order for him to learn the steps in changing his position independently.	Ashley - will provide information on changing position Alma, David and grandparents - will provide opportunities for changing position independently Denise - will act as consultant to Ashley and the family	Parents and grandparents will carry out: 1. When Ricky wants up from his back, ask him "Do you want up?" 2. Roll Ricky on his side and place his arm down. Help him push up with that arm and bear his weight on his other arm. 3. Gradually reduce assistance as Ricky gets stronger. On weekly home visits, Ashley will provide information obtained from Denise on changing positions.	10-10-89 11-24-89 12-15-89	2 3 6

Family's Evaluations:
1... Situation changed, no longer a need
2... Situation unchanged, still a need, goal or project
3... Implementation begun, still a need, goal or project
4... Outcome partially attained or accomplished
5... Outcome accomplished or attained, but not to the family's satisfaction
6... Outcome mostly accomplished or attained to the family's satisfaction
7... Outcome completely accomplished or attained to the family's satisfaction

| Name | Ricky Jones | | Family's Name | Jones | IFSP# | FIPP Staff Member | Johnson |

OPD.0

Date / #	NEED/PROJECT OUTCOME STATEMENT	SOURCE OF SUPPORT/ RESOURCE	COURSE OF ACTION	FAMILY'S EVALUATION Date	Rating
9-8 / 4	Ricky will bear weight on his feet in order to stand independently.	Ashley - will provide encouragement and information on motor skills Alma, David and grandparents - will provide opportunities for Ricky to bear weight Denise - will act as consultant to Ashley and the family	During the day, family will carry out: **1.** Pull Ricky to stand facing you; use lots of praise and social games. **2.** Hold Ricky from behind at the hips. **3.** Balance Ricky in front of sofa or chair and put toys in front of him to hold his attention. **4.** Encourage him. On weekly home visits, Ashley will share information provided by Denise about motor skills.	10-10-89 12-15-89 1-26-90	2 3 7
9-8 / 5	Ricky will learn to cruise in order to develop independent walking.	Denise - will provide information on motor skills to parents and Ashley Ashley - will model activities Parents and grandparents - will provide opportunities for cruising	Ashley will model motor activities for family on weekly home visits. Parents and grandparents will carry out suggestions at home. Denise will provide consultation.	10-24-89 11-10-89 12-11-89 1-26-90	2 3 3 4
9-10 / 6	Ricky will return to sleep on his own after waking during the night in order for David and Alma to get a full night's sleep.	Ashley - will give information, support, and make suggestions Alma and David - will support each other to carry out the suggestions consistently	Family will carry out the following: **1.** Play with Ricky between 6 & 7:30 and keep from a late afternoon nap. **2.** Give him a snack and bottle around 7:30-8 pm before bedtime. **3.** Parents reassure Ricky verbally when he awakens & fusses. **4.** Parents will wait longer before going to Ricky when he cries. On weekly home visits, Ashley and family will discuss progress and make changes.	10-10-89 11-10-89 12-4-89 1-10-90	2 3 4 7

1... Situation changed, no longer a need

Family's Evaluations: 2... Situation unchanged, still a need, goal or project
3... Implementation begun, still a need, goal or project
4... Outcome partially attained or accomplished
5... Outcome accomplished or attained, but not to the family's satisfaction
6... Outcome mostly accomplished or attained to the family's satisfaction
7... Outcome completely accomplished or attained to the family's satisfaction

Name __Ricky Jones__   OPD.0 _____   Family's Name __Jones__   IFSP# _____   FIPP Staff Member __Johnson__

Date / #	NEED/PROJECT OUTCOME STATEMENT	SOURCE OF SUPPORT/ RESOURCE	COURSE OF ACTION	FAMILY'S EVALUATION Date	Rating
11-10 / 7	Ricky will feed himself with a spoon in order to learn independent eating skills.	Ashley - will provide information on feeding and model Family members - will provide opportunities for Ricky to use a spoon in feeding	David and Alma will allow Ricky to handle spoon to eat food. Ashley will continue to check Ricky's progress on feeding when she makes several weekly visits at mealtime.	11-17-89 12-11-89 1-10-90 1-28-90	2 3 4 4
1-26 / 8	Ricky will make sounds when he gestures in order to develop the use of words.	Jackie Ward - will provide communication suggestions to Ashley Ashley - will provide information on communication Family members - will provide opportunities for Ricky to use words	Family will carry out the following: 1. When Ricky indicates what he wants by pointing, ask him, "Do you want ___?" (& supply the word). 2. When Ricky smiles or gestures, repeat the word and wait. 3. Give Ricky 10-15 seconds to respond, then repeat the word. On weekly home visits, Ashley will share communication suggestions provided by Jackie Ward.	1-30-90	3

1... Situation changed, no longer a need
2... Situation unchanged, still a need, goal or project
Family's Evaluations: 3... Implementation begun, still a need, goal or project
4... Outcome partially attained or accomplished

5... Outcome accomplished or attained, but not to the family's satisfaction
6... Outcome mostly accomplished or attained to the family's satisfaction
7... Outcome completely accomplished or attained to the family's satisfaction

Child's Name Ricky Jones   OPD.0 00-0000   Matrix #: _____

DATE STARTED	OBJECTIVES	Morning wake-up time	Play time	Mealtime	Naptime	Bathtime	Bedtime	DATE ATTAINED
		ROUTINES						
9-8-89	Ricky will get from a prone position to sitting in order to learn the steps in changing his position independently.	X	X		X		X	
9-8-89	Ricky will bear weight on his feet in order to learn independent standing.	X	X			X		1-26-90
9-8-89	Ricky will practice cruising in order to develop independent walking.		X					
10-10-89	Ricky will return to sleep after waking during the night in order for his parents to get a full night's sleep.						X	1-10-90
11-10-89	Ricky will feed himself with a spoon in order to learn independent eating skills.			X				
1-26-90	Ricky will make sounds when he gestures in order to develop the use of words.	X	X	X		X		

Stop and Practice Your Skills

Activity: Filling Out the IFSP

Choose several needs/projects currently of interest to a family you are working with (one which you have been involved with for several months), then practice filling out the blank IFSP which follows this page. Don't worry about recording dates correctly or remembering all the details of what has been done in the past.

A few helpful tips for writing IFSP's:

- There is limited space on the form, so utilize the available space to meet your individual needs.

- Goals may be added at any time during the year.

- IFSP's need not be typed.

- When appropriate, write the functional role of the case coordinator and others (e.g., resource, consultant, etc.).

- Need/project statements should include a clear outcome ("in order to...").

Western Carolina Center
Family, Infant and Preschool Program
Individualized Family Support Plan

Background Information:

Child's Name: _____

Family's Name: _____

No. OPD-0___: _____

Date of Birth: _____   Age: _____

County: _____

Family Member's Name: _____   **Relationship to Child:** _____

Family Support Plan Team

Name	Title	Agency	Date
	Parent		
	Case Coordinator		

Team Review Dates

30 Days: _____   3 Months: _____   6 Months: _____   9 Months: _____

Child's Name _____ OPD.0 _____ Family's Name _____

CHILD'S FUNCTIONING LEVEL

Domain	CA	Age Level/Range	Domain	CA	Age Level/Range

CHILD'S STRENGTHS

FAMILY'S STRENGTHS

RESOURCES AND SUPPORT SERVICES

	Dates	
	Started	Ended

RESOURCES AND SUPPORT SERVICES

	Dates	
	Started	Ended

Name _____ OPD.0 _____ Family's Name _____ IFSP# _____
FIPP Staff Member _____

Date #	NEED/PROJECT OUTCOME STATEMENT	SOURCE OF SUPPORT/ RESOURCE	COURSE OF ACTION	FAMILY'S EVALUATION	
				Date	Rating

Family's Evaluations:
1... Situation changed, no longer a need
2... Situation unchanged, still a need, goal or project
3.... Implementation begun, still a need, goal or project
4... Outcome partially attained or accomplished
5... Outcome accomplished or attained, but not to the family's satisfaction
6... Outcome mostly accomplished or attained to the family's satisfaction
7... Outcome completely accomplished or attained to the family's satisfaction

Child's Name _____	OPD.0 _____	Matrix #: _____						
DATE STARTED	OBJECTIVES	ROUTINES						DATE ATTAINED

Appendices

Appendix A: Competencies

Developing Individualized Family Support Plans

1.0   NEEDS IDENTIFICATION

    1.1   Ability to help the family define or clarify their priorities and needs.

    1.2   Ability to help the family prioritize goals.

    1.3   Ability to recognize need for help or assistance from verbal and nonverbal cues.

    1.4   Ability to respond to the perceived need and appropriately offer help.

    1.5   Ability to help the family identify needs through looking at daily routines.

    1.6   Ability to take a global developmental need (like walking) and translate that into functional skills and arrive at goals which can be used in the IFSP.

    1.7   Ability to gather information that is directly applicable to the assessment and intervention process.

    1.8   Ability or skill in using information gathered from a pencil and paper instrumentation to generate probes or interview questions to gather further necessary information.

    1.9   Ability to enable family members to gather and evaluate information.

2.0   STRENGTHS AND FAMILY FUNCTIONING

    2.1   Ability to identify family's strengths (not just individual strengths) from the family's descriptions, actions, or environment and note these strengths on the IFSP.

    2.2   Ability or skill in helping the family use a strength/resource to meet a need.

    2.3   Ability to help families see that the things they do well are strengths.

    2.4   Ability to rephrase comments made or situations described by the family in order to point out the family's strengths.

    2.5   Ability to help families understand strengths as a process, not just an outcome.

3.0 RESOURCES

    3.1   Ability to help the family identify their whole informal network.

    3.2   Ability to take a prioritized need and, with the family, identify who in the network would be a possible support source for meeting the need.

    3.3   Ability to help the family identify qualities of their network that may be facilitating or hindering their accessing supports.

    3.4   Ability to help the family expand their informal network when the current network does not have the members necessary to meet the family's needs.

    3.5   Ability to conduct family meetings in order to gather information about the complete family system which can be used in developing the IFSP.

    3.6   Ability to help a family generate options for a solution to a need or a problem.

    3.7   Ability to help the family to use their informal network first and most often in meeting needs.

    3.8   Ability to help a family identify and use formal network effectively when needed.

    3.9   Ability to develop a plan for mobilizing resources and use the plan in the IFSP.

4.0 HELP-GIVER

    4.1   Ability to conduct an interview that promotes partnership, honesty, and the family's sense of control.

    4.2   Ability to adapt quickly and respond appropriately to the changes in the family's needs.

    4.3   Ability to promote the family's acquisition of competencies and abilities while conveying to the family the sense of partnership, particularly in writing an IFSP.

    4.4   Ability to promote the family's acquisition of competencies that decrease the need for future help.

    4.5   Ability to help the family see that they have been responsible for bringing about the change.

    4.6   Ability to listen to others with understanding and empathy.

    4.7   Ability to respond supportively in emotion-laden or crisis situations.

4.8   Ability to transmit knowledge and skills to others in a manner that is enabling and empowering.

4.9   Ability to respect and appreciate individual and family differences and perspectives.

4.10   Ability to read and correctly interpret nonverbal cues from the family and observations of their environment.

4.11   Ability to use some paper/pencil instruments for identifying needs, strengths, and supports when it is appropriate for the family.

4.12   Ability to offer help that corresponds to the social and cultural perspective of the family.

4.13   Ability to act in ways which communicate to the family that the locus of decision-making clearly rests with the family.

4.14   Ability to help the family identify the pros and the cons (response cost) of seeking a particular type of help, especially when the help is coming from professionals.

4.15   Ability to allow the family to reciprocate without setting up the expectation of repayment.

4.16   Ability to identify solutions to meet needs in a way that families experience immediate success in solving their needs.

4.17   Ability to systematically increase the family's level of empowerment while providing decreased levels of help.

4.18   Ability to assist families in resolving crises which reflect conflicting needs of different family members.

5.0 FAMILY ASSESSMENT

5.1   Ability to demonstrate knowledge of the utility of the major models of parent and family functioning for assessing the parents and families of handicapped infants.

5.2   Ability to demonstrate knowledge of the various purposes of assessing parents and families of handicapped infants.

5.3   Ability to demonstrate knowledge of available assessment tools and procedures appropriate for assessing the parents and families of handicapped infants.

5.4   Ability to demonstrate knowledge of the implications of the principles of assessment for assessing parent and family functioning.

5.5 Ability to demonstrate knowledge of the determinants of outcomes of assessment of parents and families of handicapped infants.

5.6 Ability to demonstrate knowledge of the impact of atypical development on the administration and interpretation of assessment of parents and families of handicapped infants.

5.7 Ability to demonstrate knowledge of the assessments and limitations of the use of assessment procedures for assessing parents and families.

5.8 Ability to demonstrate knowledge of the utility of family level assessment information for developing and monitoring IFSP's.

5.9 Ability to demonstrate the use of the major models of parent and family functioning assessment for assessing and describing infant development and functioning.

5.10 Ability to demonstrate the use of assessment tools and procedures to accomplish the major purposes of the assessment of parents and families.

5.11 Ability to demonstrate critical evaluation of the selection, administration, and interpretation of family-level assessment tools and procedures in terms of their reliability, validity, and utility.

5.12 Ability to demonstrate the selection of appropriate assessment methods appropriate for use with parents and families with infants with different handicapping conditions.

5.13 Ability to identify, as part of the assessment process, the determinants of parent and family functioning.

5.14 Ability to demonstrate a working knowledge of the following major models for conceptualizing the assessment of parents and families:

    5.14.1 Social systems theory

    5.14.2 Family systems theory

    5.14.3 Social network theory

    5.14.4 Help-seeking theory

5.15 Ability to demonstrate knowledge of the following major purposes for assessing parent and family functioning:

    5.15.1 Screening

    5.15.2 Assessment (Edumetric)

    5.15.3 Research

5.16 Ability to demonstrate knowledge of the following major approaches to parent and family assessment:

    5.16.1   Behavioral recording

    5.16.2   Observational

    5.16.3   Rating scales

    5.16.4   Interview procedures

    5.16.5   Needs-based assessment

    5.16.6   Family strengths assessment

5.17 Ability to demonstrate knowledge of the following major types of assessment tools and procedures used to assess family and parent functioning.

    5.17.1   Family resources

    5.17.2   Social support (informal and formal)

    5.17.3   Role sharing

    5.17.4   Well-being and health

    5.17.5   Coping and management

    5.17.6   Parent belief systems (attitudes, expectations, etc.)

    5.17.7   Parent and family needs

5.18 Ability to demonstrate knowledge of the following major factors and variables that may affect assessment of parent and family functioning.

    5.18.1   Characteristics of the assessment procedures

    5.18.2   Characteristics of the parents and family

    5.18.3   Characteristics of assessment context

    5.18.4   Characteristics of assessor

    5.18.5   Characteristics of the parent/family-assessment relationship

5.19 Ability to demonstrate the appropriate use of knowledge about parent and family functioning when assessing parents and families and writing and updating the IFSP.

6.0 OTHER PROFESSIONAL AREAS

6.1 Ability to share information among professionals (internal and external) in a manner that supports the family's goals and respects confidentiality.

6.2   Ability to know when to use paper and pencil tools for assessment purposes and when to use other methods.

6.3   Ability to express to others the salient factors that influence clinical decisions when working with a family.

6.4   Ability to get help when having difficulty in dealing with a particular situation (informational and emotional).

6.5   Ability to assess one's own performance and feelings in a helping relationship, as well as to keep personal feelings and needs separate from professional relationships.

6.6   Ability to use a variety of professional roles in working with families.

6.7   Ability to assist the family in a wide range of advocacy efforts from information gathering to getting a special counsel.

6.8   Ability to acknowledge that professionals make mistakes.

6.9   Ability to demonstrate competency in development and evaluation of the IFSP.

6.10 Ability to develop objectives and document progress clearly and objectively on the IFSP.

6.11 Ability to state intended outcomes for the child in the form of behavioral objectives (state a behavior, a criterion, and a condition in observable, measurable terms).

6.12 Ability to develop strategies based on an assessment of parent/family needs for participation in the IFSP. Plan and implement a means of periodic review of child's progress.

Appendix B: Checklist

This checklist is a valuable training tool for both the trainer and the trainee. The trainer observes the trainee, then codes the trainee's performance with "✓" for demonstrated, "A" for needs assistance, or "NA" for not appropriate. Immediate specific feedback should be given verbally, to help the trainee to improve his/her performance. The trainee and trainer need to work together to practice these skills with a goal of demonstrating at least 13 of the 15 checklist competencies.

If taking the course for self-study, the trainee may use the checklists as a measuring guide by doing a self-rating. A peer could also be asked to observe and code the trainee's performance.

Trainee's Name: _____

FAMILY NEEDS

Did the trainee...

		1st observation	2nd observation	3rd observation
	Date:			
	Observer:			
1. Identify family needs?				
2. Provide feedback to the parents with regard to parent concerns or needs?				
3. Identify with the parents possible options and resources available to meet family needs?				
4. Assist the family in clarifying the need in an effort to determine the appropriate resources?				

FAMILY STRENGTHS

Did the trainee...

		1st observation	2nd observation	3rd observation
	Date:			
	Observer:			
1. Assist the family in utilizing their strengths to determine the appropriate resource?				
2. Reinforce the family for meeting their needs by utilizing their strengths?				

SCORING KEY: ✓ = demonstrated   A = needs assistance   NA = not appropriate

SUPPORT & RESOURCES

	1st observation	2nd observation	3rd observation
Date:			
Observer:			

Did the trainee...

	1st observation	2nd observation	3rd observation
1. Acknowledge the family's feelings toward using or not using a resource?			
2. Share information about other resources the family may not be aware of?			
3. Explore the outcomes of utilizing particular resources?			
4. Explore both formal and informal support options to meet the identified need?			

HELP-GIVER ROLES

	1st observation	2nd observation	3rd observation
Date:			
Observer:			

Did the trainee...

	1st observation	2nd observation	3rd observation
1. Encourage positive interaction with the parents by incorporating family strengths into the conversation or task?			
2. Respond to the parents' verbal communication and non-verbal cues in a clear and concise manner?			
3. State comments and opinions as positively as possible?			
4. Establish a relationship in which both help-giver (trainee) and parent maintain equal roles?			
5. Indicate interest in continued involvement with the parent?			

SCORING KEY: ✓ = demonstrated   A = needs assistance   NA = not appropriate

Appendix C: Portfolio Activities

Portfolio activities help trainees gain practical experience in applying knowledge and skills learned in training. The activities do not have to be "graded" in the traditional sense; however, specific feedback from the trainer on progress in applying the concepts to specific situations is very beneficial. The following list of suggested activities allow the trainees to practice new skills while taking an active role with families. The activities can be modified to fit many different training situations if necessary.

1. Administer and score the Family Functioning Style Scale with a family. Use this assessment tool as a basis for initiating conversation with the family about family strengths.

2. Interview a family for the purpose of identifying family strengths. Based on your interview, describe what qualities make this family "strong." Use the qualities of strong families in the text as a guide. Tape record your interview and critique yourself.

3. Keep a log of conversations you have with parents during "drop-off" and "pick-up" times in a center-based program. List:

   a. the needs the parent mentions to you
   b. the people/resources the parent has talked to or plans to use in some way
   c. the role that you play in helping the family meet needs

4. Meet with parents to talk about their child's progress. Identify and update the family needs/goals for their child. Help the family explore informal resources outside of school to help meet those needs.

5. Administer a support scale or complete the eco-mapping exercise with a particular family to identify their support network.

6. Choose a family and a specific need (or needs) they have mentioned. Considering your knowledge of the family and their strengths, generate a list of resources or support that may be options for meeting needs.

7. Make a list of formal resources available in your community categorized according to the services or help that the resource can provide. Organize your list under the following headings: money, food, transportation, education, home, communication, recreation, and child care.

8. Make a list of informal resources available to a family. Organize the list into categories of friends, family, neighbors, churches, etc.

9. Develop a center bulletin board or newsletter which shares information with parents regarding formal and informal support resources in the community.

10. Develop an IFSP with a family you have been working with for at least 3 months. Continue for another 3 months, utilizing the IFSP and adapting needs and projects as necessary. Do the checklists in Appendix B right after completing the IFSP.

11. Choose a family whose child is diagnosed as profoundly handicapped and whose progress may be minimal. Develop functional goals for this child, showing how you incorporated the family's needs and projects. Use the IFSP form, then do the checklists in Appendix B.

12. Choose a family you are home visiting whose child is also in a center-based program. Develop two Routines Matrices (one for home use and one for day care use), showing how the same goals can be worked on at home and at day care during normal routines of the child's day.

Appendix D: Forms

The following pages contain copies of the assessment tools and IFSP forms used in this training manual. These forms may be duplicated for further practice or for creating overhead transparencies.

Family Needs Scale

Carl J. Dunst, Carolyn S. Cooper, Janet C. Weeldreyer, Kathy D. Snyder, and Joyce H. Chase

Name_____ Date_____

> This scale asks you to indicate if you have a need for any type of help or assistance in 41 different areas. Please *circle* the response that best describes how you feel about needing help in those areas.

To what extent do you feel the need for any of the following types of help or assistance:	Not Applicable	Almost Never	Seldom	Sometimes	Often	Almost Always
1. Having money to buy necessities and pay bills	NA	1	2	3	4	5
2. Budgeting money	NA	1	2	3	4	5
3. Paying for special needs of my child	NA	1	2	3	4	5
4. Saving money for the future	NA	1	2	3	4	5
5. Having clean water to drink	NA	1	2	3	4	5
6. Having food for two meals for my family	NA	1	2	3	4	5
7. Having time to cook healthy meals for my family	NA	1	2	3	4	5
8. Feeding my child	NA	1	2	3	4	5
9. Getting a place to live	NA	1	2	3	4	5
10. Having plumbing, lighting, heat	NA	1	2	3	4	5
11. Getting furniture, clothes, toys	NA	1	2	3	4	5
12. Completing chores, repairs, home improvements	NA	1	2	3	4	5
13. Adapting my house for my child	NA	1	2	3	4	5
14. Getting a job	NA	1	2	3	4	5
15. Having a satisfying job	NA	1	2	3	4	5
16. Planning for future job of my child	NA	1	2	3	4	5
17. Getting where I need to go	NA	1	2	3	4	5
18. Getting in touch with people I need to talk to	NA	1	2	3	4	5
19. Transporting my child	NA	1	2	3	4	5
20. Having special travel equipment for my child	NA	1	2	3	4	5
21. Finding someone to talk to about my child	NA	1	2	3	4	5
22. Having someone to talk to	NA	1	2	3	4	5
23. Having medical and dental care for my family	NA	1	2	3	4	5
24. Having time to take care of myself	NA	1	2	3	4	5
25. Having emergency health care	NA	1	2	3	4	5
26. Finding special dental and medical care for my child	NA	1	2	3	4	5
27. Planning for future health needs	NA	1	2	3	4	5
28. Managing the daily needs of my child at home	NA	1	2	3	4	5
29. Caring for my child during work hours	NA	1	2	3	4	5
30. Having emergency child care	NA	1	2	3	4	5
31. Getting respite care for my child	NA	1	2	3	4	5
32. Finding care for my child in the future	NA	1	2	3	4	5
33. Finding a school placement for my child	NA	1	2	3	4	5
34. Getting equipment or therapy for my child	NA	1	2	3	4	5
35. Having time to take my child to appointments	NA	1	2	3	4	5
36. Exploring future educational options for my child	NA	1	2	3	4	5
37. Expanding my education, skills, and interests	NA	1	2	3	4	5
38. Doing things that I enjoy	NA	1	2	3	4	5
39. Doing things with my family	NA	1	2	3	4	5
40. Participation in parent groups or clubs	NA	1	2	3	4	5
41. Traveling/vacationing with my child	NA	1	2	3	4	5

Source: C.J. Dunst, C.M. Trivette, and A.G. Deal (1988). *Enabling and Empowering Families: Principles and Guidelines for Practice.* Cambridge, MA: Brookline Books. May be reproduced.

FAMILY FUNCTIONING STYLE SCALE

Angela G. Deal   Carol M. Trivette   Carl J. Dunst

Family Name _____ Date _____

INSTRUCTIONS

Every family has unique strengths and capabilities, although different families have different ways of using their abilities. This questionnaire asks you to indicate whether or not your family is characterized by 26 different qualities. The questionnaire is divided into three parts. Part 1 below asks you about all the members of your immediate family (persons living in your household). Part 2 on the inside asks you to rate the extent to which different statements are true for your family. Part 3 on the last page asks you to write down the things that you think are your family's most important strengths.

Please list all the members of your immediate family and fill in the information requested. When you are finished, turn to the next page.

FAMILY MEMBER	DATE OF BIRTH	AGE	RELATIONSHIP

Listed below are 26 statements about families. Please read each statement and indicate the extent to which it is true for your family (people living in your home). Please give your honest opinions and feelings. Remember that your family will not be like ALL the statements given.

How is your family like the following statements?	Not At All Like My Family	A Little Like My Family	Sometimes Like My Family	Usually Like My Family	Almost Always Like My Family
1. We make personal sacrifices if they help our family......................	0	1	2	3	4
2. We agree about how family members should behave...........	0	1	2	3	4
3. We believe that something good comes out of even the worst situations................................	0	1	2	3	4
4. We take pride in even the smallest accomplishments of family members............................	0	1	2	3	4
5. We share our concerns and feelings in useful ways..................	0	1	2	3	4
6. Our family sticks together no matter how difficult things get......	0	1	2	3	4
7. We can ask for help from persons outside our family if needed..	0	1	2	3	4
8. We agree about the things that are important to our family...........	0	1	2	3	4
9. We are willing to "pitch in" and help each other.............................	0	1	2	3	4
10. We find things to do that keep our minds off our worries...............	0	1	2	3	4
11. We try to look "at the bright side of things"..	0	1	2	3	4
12. We find time to be together........	0	1	2	3	4
13. Everyone in our family understands the "rules" about acceptable ways to act..............	0	1	2	3	4

How is your family like the following statements?	Not At All Like My Family	A Little Like My Family	Sometimes Like My Family	Usually Like My Family	Almost Always Like My Family
14. Friends and relatives are willing to help whenever needed.........	0	1	2	3	4
15. Our family is able to make decisions about what to do when we have problems or concerns.........................	0	1	2	3	4
16. We enjoy time together...............	0	1	2	3	4
17. We try to forget our problems or concerns for a while when they seem overwhelming....................	0	1	2	3	4
18. Family members are able to listen to both sides of the story.....	0	1	2	3	4
19. We make time to get things done that are important..............	0	1	2	3	4
20. We can depend on the support of each other when-ever something goes wrong......	0	1	2	3	4
21. We talk about the different ways we deal with problems and concerns.................................	0	1	2	3	4
22. Our family's relationships will outlast material possessions........	0	1	2	3	4
23. We make decisions like moving or changing jobs for the good of all family members....................	0	1	2	3	4
24. We can depend on each other..	0	1	2	3	4
25. We try not to take each other for granted..........................	0	1	2	3	4
26. We try to solve our problems first before asking others to help.......	0	1	2	3	4

Please write down all things that you consider to be the major strengths of your family. Don't overlook the little things that occur every day which we often take for granted (e.g., sharing the responsibility of getting your child fed and to school).

FAMILY FUNCTIONING STYLE SCALE

SCORING FORM

Angela G. Deal   Carol M. Trivette   Carl J. Dunst

Respondent _____   Date _____   Recorder _____

DIRECTIONS
The scoring process is designed to facilitate accurate summarization of responses on The Family Functioning Style Scale. The scoring sheet includes spaces for individual item scores and subscale scores. The recorder should first enter the item scores (from the Family Functioning Style Scale) in the boxes on the scoring sheet and then sum each column to obtain the subscale scores. The subscale scores are written in the top "triangle" at the bottom of each column and compared to the total possible for each column.

SCORING FORM

ITEM	Commitment	Cohesion	Communication	Competence	Coping
1		□			
2				□	
3			□		
4		□			
5			□		
6		□			
7					□
8			□		
9	□				
10					□
11					□
12	□				
13					□
14					□
15					□
16	□				
17			□		
18			□		
19	□				
20				□	
21			□		
22		□			
23		□			
24		□			
25	□				
26				□	
Subscale Score / Total Possible	20	24	24	12	24

PERSONAL NETWORK MATRIX

(Version 2)

Carol M. Trivette & Carl J. Dunst

Name_____ Date_____

This questionnaire asks about people and groups that may provide you help and assistance. The scale is divided into three parts. Please read the instructions that go with each part before completing each section of the questionnaire.

Listed below are different individuals and groups that people often have contact with face-to-face, in a group, or by telephone. Please indicate for each source listed how often you have been in contact with each person or group during the **past month**. Please indicate any person or group with whom you have had contact not included on our list.

How frequently have you had contact with each of the following during the **past month**	Not At All	Once Or Twice	Up To 10 Times	Up To 20 Times	Almost Every Day
1. Spouse or Partner	1	2	3	4	5
2. My Children	1	2	3	4	5
3. My Parents	1	2	3	4	5
4. Spouse or Partner's Parents	1	2	3	4	5
5. My Sister/Brother	1	2	3	4	5
6. Spouse or Partner's Sister/Brother	1	2	3	4	5
7. Other Relatives	1	2	3	4	5
8. Friends	1	2	3	4	5
9. Neighbors	1	2	3	4	5
10. Church Members	1	2	3	4	5
11. Minister, Priest, or Rabbi	1	2	3	4	5
12. Co-Workers	1	2	3	4	5
13. Baby Sitter	1	2	3	4	5
14. Day Care or School	1	2	3	4	5
15. Private Therapist for Child	1	2	3	4	5
16. Child/Family Doctors	1	2	3	4	5
17. Early Childhood Intervention Program	1	2	3	4	5
18. Hospital/Special Clinics	1	2	3	4	5
19. Health Department	1	2	3	4	5
20. Social Service Department	1	2	3	4	5
21. Other Agencies	1	2	3	4	5
22. _____	1	2	3	4	5
23. _____	1	2	3	4	5

Source: C.J. Dunst, C.M. Trivette, and A.G. Deal (1988). *Enabling and Empowering Families: Principles and Guidelines for Practice.* Cambridge, MA: Brookline Books. May be reproduced.

This part of the scale asks you to do two things: (1) Begin by listing up to 10 needs or activities that are of concern to you. We call these things projects because they require our time and energy. Projects include things like finding a job, paying the bills, finishing school, playing with our children, going on vacation, teaching our child how to eat, and so on. (2) After you have listed up to 10

Which person or groups to the right would you go to for help with any of these projects: **PROJECTS**	Myself	Spouse or Partner	My Children	My Parents	Spouse or Partner's Parents	Sister/ Brother	Spouse or Partner's Sister/ Brother	Other Relatives
1.								
2.								
3.								
4.								
5.								
6.								
7.								
8.								
9.								
10.								

INSTRUCTIONS

projects, please indicate which persons or groups you could go to if you need help with any of the projects. Indicate who would provide you help by checking the appropriate box for the person or group that you would ask.

Friends	Neighbors	Church Members/ Minister	Co-Workers	Babysitter, Day Care, or School	Private Therapist for Child	Child/ Family Doctors	Early Childhood Intervention Program	Health Depart.	Social Services Depart.	Other Agencies

Whenever a person needs help or assistance, he or she generally can depend upon certain persons or groups more than others. Listed below are different individuals, groups, and agencies that you might ask for help or assistance. For each source listed, please indicate to what extent you could depend upon each person or group if you needed any type of help.

To what extent can you depend upon any of the following for help or assistance when you need it:	Not At All	Some times	Occa-sionally	Most of the Time	All of the Time
1. Spouse or Partner	1	2	3	4	5
2. My Children	1	2	3	4	5
3. My Parents	1	2	3	4	5
4. Spouse or Partner's Parents	1	2	3	4	5
5. My Sister/Brother	1	2	3	4	5
6. Spouse or Partner's Sister/Brother	1	2	3	4	5
7. Other Relatives	1	2	3	4	5
8. Friends	1	2	3	4	5
9. Neighbors	1	2	3	4	5
10. Church Members	1	2	3	4	5
11. Minister, Priest, or Rabbi	1	2	3	4	5
12. Co-Workers	1	2	3	4	5
13. Baby Sitter	1	2	3	4	5
14. Day Care or School	1	2	3	4	5
15. Private Therapist for Child	1	2	3	4	5
16. Child/Family Doctors	1	2	3	4	5
17. Early Childhood Intervention Program	1	2	3	4	5
18. Hospital/Special Clinics	1	2	3	4	5
19. Health Department	1	2	3	4	5
20. Social Service Department	1	2	3	4	5
21. Other Agencies	1	2	3	4	5
22. _____	1	2	3	4	5
23. _____	1	2	3	4	5

Source: C.J. Dunst, C.M. Trivette, and A.G. Deal (1988). *Enabling and Empowering Families: Principles and Guidelines for Practice.* Cambridge, MA: Brookline Books. May be reproduced.

Western Carolina Center
Family, Infant and Preschool Program
Individualized Family Support Plan

Background Information:

Child's Name: _____

Family's Name: _____

No. OPD-0___: _____   Age: _____

Date of Birth: _____

County: _____

Family Member's Name:

Relationship to Child:

Family Support Plan Team

Name	Title	Agency	Date
	Parent		
	Case Coordinator		

Team Review Dates

30 Days: _____   3 Months: _____   6 Months: _____   9 Months: _____

Child's Name _____ OPD.0 _____ Family's Name _____

CHILD'S FUNCTIONING LEVEL

Domain	CA	Age Level/Range	Domain	CA	Age Level/Range

CHILD'S STRENGTHS

FAMILY'S STRENGTHS

RESOURCES AND SUPPORT SERVICES

Resources and Support Services	Dates	
	Started	Ended

RESOURCES AND SUPPORT SERVICES

Resources and Support Services	Dates	
	Started	Ended

Name _____ OPD.0 _____ Family's Name _____ IFSP# _____ FIPP Staff Member _____

Date #	NEED/PROJECT OUTCOME STATEMENT	SOURCE OF SUPPORT/ RESOURCE	COURSE OF ACTION	FAMILY'S EVALUATION Date	Rating

Family's Evaluations:
1... Situation changed, no longer a need
2... Situation unchanged, still a need, goal or project
3... Implementation begun, still a need, goal or project
4... Outcome partially attained or accomplished
5... Outcome accomplished or attained, but not to the family's satisfaction
6... Outcome mostly accomplished or attained to the family's satisfaction
7... Outcome completely accomplished or attained to the family's satisfaction

Child's Name _____		OPD.0 _____	Matrix #: _____							
				ROUTINES						DATE ATTAINED
DATE STARTED	OBJECTIVES									

Appendix E: Overhead Transparency Masters

The following pages contain masters for creating overhead transparencies to be used in seminar. These overhead transparencies should be prepared in advance of the training sessions.

Family-Level Assessment & Intervention Principles

SECTION	ASSESSMENT/INTERVENTION PRINCIPLE	IMPLEMENTATION
Needs & Aspirations	SPECIFICATION AND PRIORITIZATION OF FAMILY NEEDS AND ASPIRATIONS	Use needs-based assessment strategies and interviews to identify the needs and goals the family is willing to devote time and energy toward meeting and achieving.
Strengths & Capabilities	UTILIZATION OF EXISTING FAMILY STRENGTHS AND CAPABILITIES	Identify existing family strengths and skills which can be applied to meet present needs, as well as strengths which need to be developed to increase independence and self-reliance.
Support & Resources	IDENTIFICATION OF SOURCES OF SUPPORT AND RESOURCES FOR MEETING NEEDS AND ACHIEVING ASPIRATIONS	Use the procedure of "mapping" to identify both existing and potential sources of support and resources from among the family's personal social network.
The Effective Help-Giver	CREATION OF OPPORTUNITIES FOR THE DEVELOPMENT OF ADDITIONAL SKILLS AND COMPETENCIES	Employ helping behaviors and strategies which create opportunities for the family to develop a wide variety of abilities to meet needs and achieve desired goals.

Needs Assessment Interview Procedures

◇ Be positive; take the lead in setting up the initial interview

- Clearly state the reason you'd like to visit with the family

- Establish a positive, non-threatening atmosphere

- Encourage the participation of all family members

- Arrange for the interview in a place familiar to the family

◇ First get to know the family and put them at ease

- Learn each person's name and all family relationships

- Chat with each person and express "thanks" for participation

◇ Clearly state the purpose of the interview

- Stress that this is the family's meeting -- the agenda is their's

- Explain your role as a learner and partner

<u>Needs Assessment Interview Procedures --2</u>

◇ Listen to and record family needs and family goals

- Let the family "tell its story;" pay attention to each member

- Make written or mental notes about needs and goals

◇ Help the family clarify concerns and needs

- Use good listening skills and ask for needed clarification

- As you understand the reasons for needs, be prepared to redefine them

◇ Be an empathic, responsive, active listener throughout the interview

- Be sensitive to verbal and non-verbal messages

- Use techniques like active and reflective listening, open-ended questions

◇ Establish consensus regarding priority needs and goals

- Restate family-identified needs and goals

- Help the family achieve consensus prioritizing needs and goals

EFFECTIVE INTERVIEWING

OBSERVE

* ❖ Behavior of family members

* ❖ Physical environment

ASK

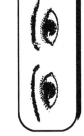

???

* ❖ About daily routines

* ❖ Questions about strengths

LISTEN

* ❖ Actively, looking for clues

* ❖ Carefully, communicating empathy

STATE

xxx xxxxx xxx

* ❖ Negative points in a positive way

* ❖ Strengths that you observe

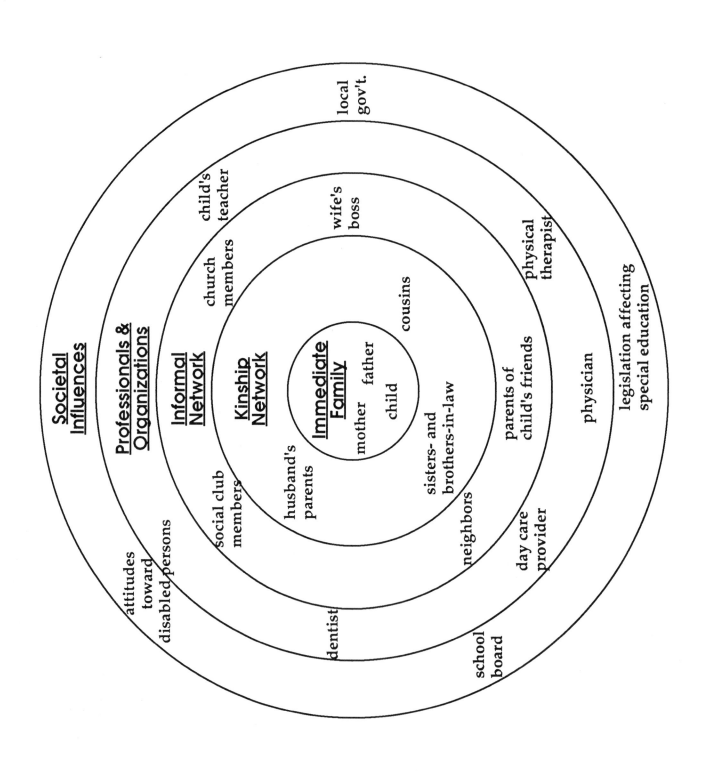

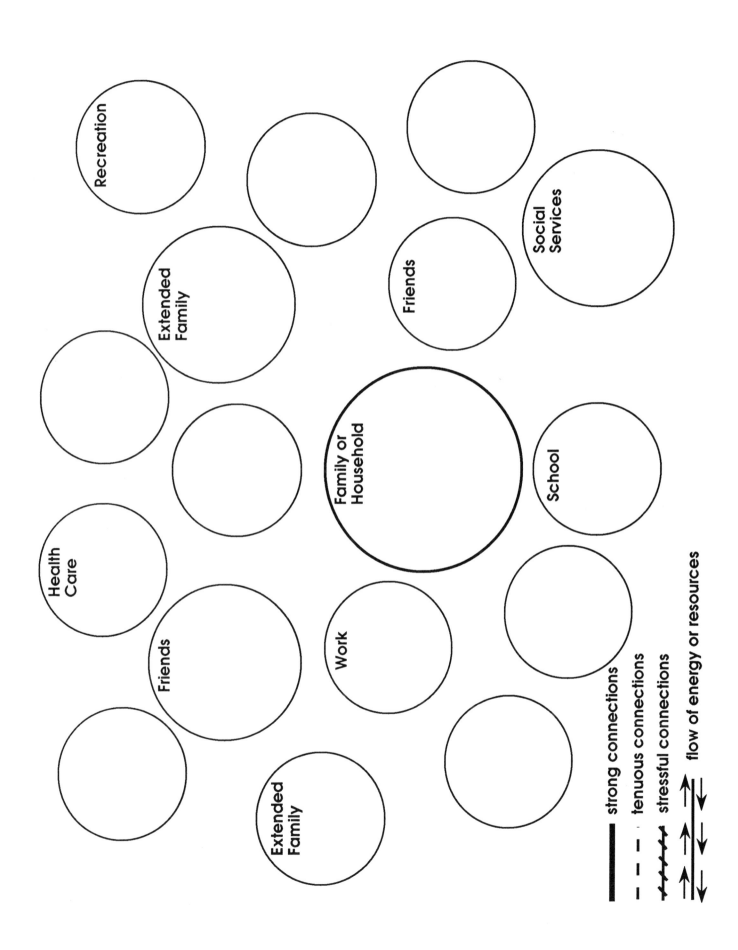

Recreation

Extended Family

Friends

Social Services

Health Care

Family or Household

School

Friends

Work

Extended Family

strong connections

tenuous connections

stressful connections

flow of energy or resources

Appendix F: Glossary

Adaptability: The ability of the family to change in response to situational and developmental change.

Balanced Families: Stable families that have flexible role relationships.

Chaotic Families: Families that are continually unstable, with relationship rules which are in flux, in which no one appears to be in charge (from family systems theory).

Close Families: Families with strong affectionate ties to one another, but which also allow individuals to be autonomous.

Cohesion: The degree of closeness or distance among family members; the emotional bonding members have toward one another.

Cohesive (or Caring) Families: Families that have strong affectionate ties to one another.

Combination of Competencies: Two or more family members performing the same or similar tasks to achieve a desired goal (e.g., all family members "chipping in" and cleaning the house before visitors arrive).

Commonality: The time, space, interest, activities and friends shared by family members.

Communication: The process by which information is exchanged and transmitted in families; perhaps the most important element in family dynamics; effective communication includes 1) sending clear messages, 2) listening, and 3) providing feedback.

Disengaged Families: Families with little closeness or support for one another (from family systems theory).

Effective Helping: The act of enabling individuals or groups (e.g., families) to become better able to solve problems, meet needs, or achieve aspirations by promoting acquisition of competencies that support and strengthen functioning in a way that permits a greater sense of individual or group control over its developmental course.

Empowerment: 1.) A family's ability to meet needs and achieve aspirations in a way that promotes a clear sense of intrafamily mastery and control over important aspects of family functioning. 2.) Carrying out interventions in a manner in which family members acquire a sense of control over their lives as a result of their efforts to meet needs. 3.) Empowerment implies that many competencies are already present or at least possible. Empowerment implies that what you see as poor functioning is a result of social structure and lack of resources which make it impossible for the existing competencies to operate. It implies that in those cases where new information needs to be learned, it is better learned in a context of living life rather than in artificial programs.

Enabling: 1.) Creating opportunities for all family members to display and acquire competencies that strengthen family functioning. 2.) Creating opportunities for family members to become more competent, independent, and self-sustaining with respect to their abilities to mobilize their social networks to get needs met and attain desired goals.

Enhancing the Acquisition of Competencies: Providing families with the information and skills necessary to be more self-sustaining and thus better able to promote personal well-being as well as have positive influences in other areas of family functioning.

Enmeshed Families: Families whose members exhibit little or no individual autonomy, families that are too cohesive (from family systems theory).

Family Functions: The tangible and intangible contributions the family makes which provide for the family's needs (e.g., economic, educational -- from family systems theory).

Family Functioning Style: The combination of a family's strengths and abilities to meet the needs of daily life.

Family Interaction: The process of interaction among families, governed by the family's level of cohesion, adaptability, and communication style (from family systems theory).

Family Infant and Preschool Program (FIPP): A program of the Western Carolina Center in Morganton, NC; the developers of the Individualized Family Support Plan.

Family Life Cycle: A progression of developmental and non-developmental changes which may alter family structure and family needs (from family systems theory).

Family Strengths; Relationships, skills and other characteristics of a family which encourage development of individual family members and which promote positive interaction among family members, making family life satisfying and contributing to positive family functioning.

Family Structure: The descriptive characteristics of the family, including the nature of its membership and its cultural and ideological style (from family systems theory).

Family Systems Theory: A philosophy that focuses on interactions among family members rather than on individuals within the family.

Flexible Families: Families which have flexible role relationships and flexible relationship rules.

Helping: The art of promoting and supporting family functioning in a way that enhances the acquisition of competencies, which in turn permits a greater degree of intrafamily control over subsequent activities.

Individualized Family Service Plan (IFSP): An early intervention plan for families with handicapped infant and preschool children, as described by Public Law 99-457.

Individualized Family Support Plan (IFSP): An alternative to the PL 99-457's IFSP (above), as described by the research staff at the Family, Infant and Preschool Program at the Western Carolina Center, Morganton, NC.

Interaction of Competencies: Two or more family members performing different tasks to make the family system work in the best interest of individual family members and the family as a whole.

Proactive Approach: A proactive approach to helping relationships views families -- all families -- in a positive light and places major emphasis on promoting the acquisition of self-sustaining and adaptive behaviors that emphasize growth for all family members and not just an individual child.

Rigid Families: Families where members believe people will not act responsibly without a high degree of control and structure; families that are unable to change (from family systems theory).

Social Systems Perspective: A social systems perspective views a family as a social unit embedded within other formal and informal social units and networks. It also views these different social networks as interdependent, where events and changes in one unit resonate and in turn directly and indirectly influence the behavior of individuals in other units. A social systems perspective also considers events within and between social units as supportive and health promoting to the extent that they have positive influences on family functioning.

Strengthening Families: Supporting and building upon the things the family already does well as a basis for promoting and encouraging the mobilization of resources among the family's network members.

Subsystems: The four major subsystems within the nuclear family are 1) marital (husband/wife), 2) parental (child/parent), 3) sibling (child/child), and 4) extrafamilial (whole family or individual member interactions with extended family, friends, neighbors, community, and professionals).

Supplemental Security Income (SSI): Monetary aid available to handicapped persons.

References

References

Developing Individualized Family Support Plans

Bronfenbrenner, U. (1979). *The ecology of human development: Experiments by nature and design.* Cambridge: Harvard University Press.

Curran, D. (1983). *Traits of a healthy family.* Minneapolis, MN: Winston Press.

Deal, A.G., Dunst, C.J., & Trivette, C.M. (April, 1979). A flexible and functional approach to developing IFSP's. *Infants and Young Children 1* (4), 32-43.

Deal, A.G., Trivette, C.M., & Dunst, C.J. (unpublished scale). Family Functioning Style Scale.

Dunst, C.J., & Trivette, C.M. (1987). Enabling and empowering families: Conceptual and intervention issues. *School Psychology Review, 16*(4), 443-456.

Dunst, C.J., & Trivette, C.M. (1988). Helping, helplessness, and harm. In J.C. Witt, S.M. Elliot, & F.M. Gresham (Eds.) (pp. 343-376). *Handbook of behavior therapy in education.* New York: Plenum Press.

Dunst, C.J., Trivette, C.M., Davis, M., & Cornwell, J. (1988). Enabling and empowering families of children with health impairments. *Children's Health Care, 17* (2), 71-81.

Dunst, C.J., Trivette, C.M. & Deal, A.G. (1988). *Enabling and empowering families: Principles and guidelines for practice.* Cambridge, MA: Brookline Books.

Fisher, J.D., Nadler, A., & DePaulo, B.M. (Eds.). (1983). *New directions in helping: Vol. 1. Recipient reactions to aid.* New York: Academic Press.

Fisher, J.D., Nadler, A., & Whitcher-Alagna, S. (1983). Four theoretical approaches for conceptualizing reactions to aid. In J.D. Fisher, Nadler, A., & DePaulo, B.M. (Eds.). *New directions in helping: Vol. 1. Recipient reactions to aid.* New York: Academic Press.

Garbarino, J. (1982). *Children and families in the social environment.* New York: Family Service Association of America.

Hartman, A., & Laird, J. (1983). *Family-centered social work practice.* New York: Free Press.

Hawkins. (1986). *Education of the handicapped act amendments of 1986* (Report No. 99-860). Washington, DC: 99th Congress, House of Representatives, Committee on Education and Labor.

Hill, R. (1971). *The strengths of black families.* New York: Emerson Hall.

Hobbs, N. (1975). *The futures of children: Categories, labels and their consequences.* San Francisco: Jossey-Bass.

Knowles, M.S. (1972). *The modern practice of adult education.* New York: Association Press.

Knowles, M.S. (1984). *The adult learner (3rd edition).* Houston, TX: Gulf.

Lewis, J.M., Beavers, W.R., Gossett, J.T., & Phillips, V.A. (1976). *No single thread: Psychological health in family systems.* New York: Brunner/Mazel.

Maslow, A. (1954). *Motivation and personality.* New York: Harper and Row.

Otto, H.A. (1962). What is a strong family? *Marriage and Family Living,* 24, 77-81.

Otto, H.A. (1963). Criteria for assessing family strengths. *Family Process,* 2, 329-334.

Otto, H.A. (1975). *The use of family strength concepts and methods in family life education: A handbook.* Beverly Hills, CA: The Holistic Press.

Sakata, R.T. (1984). *Adult education theory and practice* (Outreach Series Paper, Contract no. 300-82-0369). Chapel Hill, NC: Technical Assistance Development System (TADS).

Satir, V. (1972). *Peoplemaking.* Palo Alto, CA: Science and Behavior Books.

Stinnett, N., & DeFrain, J. (1985b). Family Strengths Inventory. In N. Stinnett & J. DeFrain (Eds.) *Secrets of strong families (pp 180-182).* New York: Berkley Books.

Stoneman, Z. (1985). Family involvement in early childhood special education programs. In N.H. Fallen & W. Umansky (Eds.). *Young children with special needs* (2nd ed.) (pp. 442-469). Columbus, OH: Charles E. Merrill.

Thomas, W.I., & Thomas, D.S. (1928). *The child in America.* New York: Alfred Knopp Publishing Company.

Trivette, C.M., Dunst, C.J., Deal, A.G., Hamer, A.W., & Propst, S. (in press). Assessing family strengths and family functioning style. *Topics in Early Childhood Special Education.*

Turnbull, A.P., Summers, J.A. & Brotherson, M.J. (1984). *Working with families with disabled members: A family systems approach.* Unpublished manuscript, University of Kansas, Kansas University Affiliated Program, Lawrence.

Ward, L.D. (1983, November). Warm fuzzies vs. hard facts: Four styles of adult learning. *Training,* pp. 31-33.

Williams, R., Lindgren, H., Rowe, G. Van Zandt, S., & Stinnett, N. (Eds.). (1985). *Family strengths 6: Enhancement of interaction.* Lincoln, NE: Department of Human Development and the Family, Center for Family Strengths, University of Nebraska.